Insider's Guide to Internet Gambling

A Scoblete Get-the-Edge Guide

Insider's Guide to Internet Gambling

Your Sourcebook for Safe and Profitable Gambling
(Special Section on Horse Racing)

by John G. Brokopp

Foreword by Frank Scoblete

Bonus Books, Inc.
Chicago, Illinois

05 04 03 02 01   5 4 3 2 1

Library of Congress Card Number: 2001093749
ISBN: 1-56625-161-3

Bonus Books, Inc.
160 East Illinois Street
Chicago, Illinois 60611

Printed in the United States of America

For my children, Hollie, Lauren, Jonathan and Joshua,
And in loving memory of my father, John William Brokopp

Table of Contents

Section 2

Acknowledgments

Researching and completing a project like this cannot be possible without the encouragement and support of family and friends. I am therefore grateful to my wife, Georgette, who managed to put up with me along with giving birth to Joshua William on June 29, 2000. Being a wife and mother of four, along with putting her RN degree to valuable use as a Director of Nursing, is no small accomplishment in itself and I thank her for her patience and understanding.

As was the case with *Thrifty Gambling*, I also owe heartfelt thanks and appreciation to Charles W. Bidwill, III, "C-3," president of Sportsman's Park and chairman of the board of Chicago Motor Speedway, without whose support this book could never have been written. Charlie, everyone should have a boss as generous as you, and everyone should work for a family owned and operated organization as great as the National Jockey Club.

Thanks to Bonus Books, Inc., especially to my publisher, Aaron Cohodes, and editor Devon Freeny, and to Frank Scoblete, America's most popular gaming writer, under whose "Scoblete Get-The-Edge Guides" imprint this book is written. Frank's input and editing were invaluable resources, but it was his career hallmark of never settling for anything less than the best that made this the complete and thorough project that it became.

I am indebted to the editors I work with in conjunction with my gambling columns and features, including features editor George Haas and assistant features editor Elizabeth Kaufman of the *Daily Southtown* in Chicago, Ill.; publisher Kelly Luvison and editor Andy Thompson of *The Evening Tribune* in Hornell, N.Y.; editor Allison St. Claire of *Senior Wire Syndicate* in Denver, Co.; managing editor Mike Bailey and features editor Dave Gathman of *The Courier News* in Elgin, Ill.; publisher Catherine Jaeger and editor John Robert Busam of *Midwest Gaming & Travel* magazine; and managing editor Buster Phillips of *Chance: The Best of Gaming* magazine.

My sincere thanks go to my fellow casino gambling writers and to Internet gambling authorities nationwide who proved to be invaluable resources for gathering information and facts for this book. Their continued dedication to supplying online casino gamblers with the best information possible ranks as the sole system of checks and balances for this unregulated and undefined multi-million dollar industry.

As for the horse racing sections in this book, I am grateful to my mentors and the many co-workers, friends, colleagues and associates that I have come to know and love during my 29-year professional career as a publicist, writer and handicapper in the sport of thoroughbred racing. I hope some of the knowledge and insight that they have shared, and the experiences we have all enjoyed, will help players in their new journey into watching and betting the races online.

Special thanks go to Dave Gutfreund, one of the nation's most respected thoroughbred horse racing handicappers, who shared with me for this book his thoughts and offered his advice about the best way to approach the brave new world of betting the races. I'm sure you will find his contributions to be most interesting.

Last but hardly least, warm good wishes to my fellow casino gamblers and all those interested in gambling on the

Internet. It is my hope and desire that I have given you the guidance necessary to make your journey into cyberspace casinos a pleasant and profitable one.

Foreword

by Frank Scoblete

I went to sleep in 1971 and I woke up in the future. It is a world where everyone—or almost everyone—I know has his own computer; a relatively small contraption compared to the room-sized computers that would run amok in the best science fiction movies of my former life. ("I'm sorry, Dave, I can't open the pod bay doors. And I'm going to have to kill you and all the inhabitants of earth as well.")

It is a world where just about everyone carries around with them little phones so that they can force everyone else around them to listen to their inane conversations ("Hi, Steph, so whatcha doin'?"), or, while driving their tank-like SUVs, we are treated to the sight of them jabbering away as they go off the road or into oncoming traffic ("Scotty, beam me up," indeed!). It is a world where people pierce themselves with ugly pieces of metal because it's considered "cool"—pierce areas that in earlier times weren't even talked about, much less punctured—and where everyone craves to be different in the exact same ways with the exact same neon hair dyes. A world where sex has been discovered for the gazillionth time by a new generation who thinks the old generation is too repressed (Kids, kids, "birds do it, bees do it, even educated fleas do it" so what makes you think you discovered it?). The new world is a world where germs thrive and reason is at a premium.

This new world of the future (boy, what a long sleep it's been) is a world where just about everyone can find out just about anything about just about everyone and anything they want just by turning on a switch, playing with a mouse (not the kind that brought plagues, but a plastic kind with a very long tail and no eyes), getting onto something *ominously* called "the world wide web" and going to "sites" that exist God-knows-where in something called "cyberspace." Karl Marx would become a Republican if he realized that there might not be any end to the resources of such a world. The Church might blanche at the new meaning of "world without end" as well. The opium of the people is no longer religion, politics or opium, for that matter—it's a computer in every house and every school and every office and briefcase. It's sitting mesmerized before a screen.

Of course, such a world has all the things people have always wanted at the click of whatever it is that clicks on those machines—reams of pornography, celebrity gossip and graphic pictures of wrecks, human and otherwise.

This new world also offers us something important as well—the opportunity to gamble! After all, the words of Descartes, that great French faro player, still ring out as loudly today as they did whenever he was shouting them: "I gamble therefore I am!"

Thus the need for this book.

Out there are people such as myself, who have awakened from a long sleep, only to find that their kids exist in another time-frame altogether, that those same kids have alien-looking friends (hybrids of our space-brothers and your brother-in-law, by the looks of them), and talk a language of gigabytes, rams, modems and floppy disks. Those kids probably don't need this book for two reasons—they already know all the great websites in the universe of cyberspace and most of them can't read.

But I need it. And if you bought this book, you evidently need it too. This future world is a treacherous place, filled with charlatans and rip-off artists. And that's just in the public schools and universities. In cyberspace, anything goes, and the last thing you want going is your money to some unscrupulous cyber-casino owner whose famous saying is: "You bet it, we'll book it, and then we'll really book it—right outta town!"

So before you read any further, I say give a round of applause to the author of this book, Mr. John Brokopp, who has done a yeoman's job of sifting through an awful lot of dreck on the web to give us solid information about which gambling sites to look into and which gambling sites to stay out of.

For those of you who enjoy horse racing, he has done an additionally wonderful job in explaining why horse racing is a good bet for knowledgeable individuals and where to find the best type of information to make those good bets.

Okay, so much for Brokopp, now back to ME.

I know nothing about online casinos. I don't play online. I don't play online for three reasons:

1. I am in front of my computer all day long and to then sit in front of that same computer again when my work day is over is not an appealing thought.

2. My server is extremely old (a few years!) and really can't maneuver around the web very well. I can't even get onto my own site *www.scoblete.com*. Basically I use my computer to write and to send e-mails and receive spam (junk e-mails) about "hot Russian babes who bare it all."

3. I personally like to gamble in casinos. I like the interaction with people. I like the smell of the smoke and adrenaline (yes, I think we can *smell* the adrenaline). I like the sound of the people screaming at the slots and at their spouses for losing so much at the slots. I like the cheers from the craps tables.

But I also realize that I am fast becoming an anachronism. According to my neighbor's purple-haired, pin-cushioned kid, I am fast becoming a fossil. The Internet is where it's happening in the gambling world. I know this. People just love to gamble, and if they can gamble in the privacy of their own homes after a hard day on their cell phones, why, so much the better. But that isn't always good *for* the *bettor*.

How can you tell a good casino from a bad casino—online that is? How do you know the casino you're giving your credit card to isn't run by the Caribbean Island equivalent of Joey Soprano or Don Corleone?

If you are not an expert in online gambling, this book can help you maneuver your way through treacherous waters. Online gambling can be the Great White Shark waiting to gobble your bankbook in one or two gulps. Or it can be a manageable pastime, like keeping tropical fish.

What will make it one or the other is simple—how much knowledge you have.

And that's why you should take your time and really, really listen to what Mr. Brokopp has to say.

Section 1

Gambling's New Frontier

In the not too distant past, the only place in the United States to participate in legal casino gambling was the state of Nevada. This meant a long journey for a majority of Americans with the itch to gamble, a once-a-year vacation perhaps, or maybe taking advantage of a reasonable air and hotel package for an occasional getaway.

Atlantic City, New Jersey, joined Nevada in 1978 as only the second legalized casino gambling jurisdiction in this country. Thirteen years later, Iowa became the first state to have riverboat casino gambling. In the ensuing decade, numerous other states approved riverboat gambling legislation.

The Indian Gaming Regulatory Act of 1988 paved the way for American tribes to establish casinos, lotteries and bingo halls on tribal land in 30 states. Today more than 500 such casinos have been opened across the country.

Gambling regulation in the United States has traditionally been the domain of state governments. Hawaii and Utah are the only states that prohibit all forms of gambling. The other 48 states permit gambling of some form, be it pari-mutuel wagering on horse racing or dog racing, bingo, lotteries or, of course, casino gambling.

Casino gambling has evolved into an acceptable leisure time activity for many Americans. It can be a rewarding entertainment option. All variations of entertainment cost a lot of money these days. Casino gambling is the one option that offers the very real possibility of a positive return on your monetary investment if either luck, or the mathematical advantage coupled with good common sense are on your side.

Table games, slot machines and video poker went from being a long distance pursuit to something in which a majority of Americans can participate on a regular basis if they so desire. Just as quickly as casino gambling was introduced to virtually every region of the country, so has it become available in the comfort and privacy of homes, offices and places of business, all thanks to the Internet.

The Information Superhighway has revolutionized the way we communicate with one another, make purchases, entertain ourselves and conduct business. Anyone with a personal computer and an Internet connection can participate in any number of activities worldwide at the mere touch of a button. Casino gambling is one of those activities.

There is still much to be acted upon when it comes to this new frontier of gambling. The Interstate Wire Act of 1961 prohibits the use of telephone and telegraph communications facilities for the placing of bets on sporting events. The Internet may not even have been a glimmer in the eye of even the most technological visionary back then. Its legality is still being debated.

Bringing gambling into homes via the Internet was inevitable, even though it has happened so quickly that there are no internal government regulations or sanctions in place at the present time to oversee what has become a multi-billion dollar industry. Wherever there is money to be made in the amounts casino gambling makes possible, there are bound to be entrepreneurs to capitalize on the situation.

In some respects, Internet casinos have a big economic advantage over their land-based counterparts. Internet casinos exist in a virtual-reality world housed in a computer. Land-based casinos have employees to pay, buildings to keep up and property taxes to pay.

Internet wagering began in Australia in 1997 through NetTAB, which was originally owned and operated by the New South Wales State government. By year's end there were 40 gambling websites worldwide. Today there are more than 1,000 e-gambling properties owned and operated by any one of some 250 companies classified as either owner/operators or software suppliers.

With this fact in mind, gambling on the Internet brings with it many caveats. It can be an entertaining gambling option allowing you privacy and convenience that none of us would have thought possible several short years ago. But it can also be a demon in angel's clothing if you do not exercise the proper self-control and do the necessary investigative work.

After all, in exchange for the privacy and convenience that you can enjoy by gambling on the Internet, you must surrender a certain degree of your privacy in the form of personal information about yourself. This always carries a risk. There is also a mutual-trust factor inherent in gambling on the Internet, and more often than not the balance is tipped in favor of the casino.

When you are gambling in a casino and dealing with live people, the transfer of funds is instantaneous, bonded and guaranteed under the license of the state which sanctions it. When you gamble on an Internet casino, you are obligated to have your funds on account, but you are at the mercy of the casino to make good on their end of the bargain by giving you any winnings.

In a vast majority of cases, Internet casinos conduct their business with honor and integrity, even though at the present time there is no United States government regulation holding them to that standard. The bottom line is that they want to stay in business, and all it takes is bad publicity or word of mouth from dissatisfied customers and they'll begin to fall out of favor or even go under.

There are literally hundreds of Internet gambling casinos available. They're not all the same. Some are better than others, and it's up to you as a consumer to know what to look for when it comes to choosing a site on which to play. Some of the differences are very subtle, others quite obvious. In many cases, they are all very similar. But there are ways to find the best odds, the best games and the most reliable sites, just as there are ways to shop for the best deals in real casinos.

That will be the mission of this book. Gambling on the Internet is literally a 500-pound, out-of-control, baby gorilla. It is still in its infancy as an entertainment option and as a business, but it has grown to monstrous proportions in a very short period of time, unbridled by rules, regulations or even the approval of the United States government. Politicians are in a quandary as to what to do and how to do it. In the meantime, millions of Internet consumers worldwide are rolling the dice.

Just What Is an Online Casino?

An online casino is just like any other Internet business. You get to the casino by punching in a URL address on the keyboard of your personal computer. There are three different ways to gain access to gambling on the Internet, depending on which casino you choose.

The first way is to download the program on the hard drive of your computer. This option is made available free of charge by the online casino with which you are dealing. This download can either be done through the use of a CD-ROM or directly over the Internet. In either case, there is a certain amount of time required to download the application on your computer. Once it's in there, however, your investment of time is over, and you can play at that casino any time you desire. The programs are for the most part the most sophisticated in the way of graphics, sound and animation, all of which you should take into consideration when choosing a site.

Some online casinos use what is known as the JAVA format. Such a site does not require you to download the application on your own computer's hard drive. The online casino's applets run through your computer's browser. Whatever time you save initially you pay for in quality of sound, animation, and graphics, although they are all quite acceptable depending, of course, on the priority you place on special effects.

Then there are the casinos that use the instant gratification of HTML. Just sign up, get funds in your account, and away you go. Everything you need to gamble is right there for you a mouse click away. You're not going to have the sophisticated graphics and animation of a casino that you download, but if speed of play is what you are looking for without a lot of virtual experience, HTML casinos are for you.

The specifications of your computer come into play when you choose to gamble interactively on the Internet. Here again, technology is changing and advancing at a lightning-quick pace. Computers that were used in the early to mid-nineties are already outdated and not compatible with the demands an Internet casino requires.

Chances are the computer you currently have in your possession will be perfectly compatible for Internet gambling. The newer it is, the better, however. As for the degree of computer literacy that will be required of you in order to gamble on an online casino, you don't need to feel that you have to be a Bill Gates Junior to be effective and efficient. Anybody with any degree of experience working with a computer and connecting to the Internet can be most proficient at working his or her way around the online casino. It isn't rocket science.

The more experience you have, the better. That's why it can be beneficial if you find a casino that will allow you to play for fun just to get a little experience and expertise. That's the best way to go prior to putting your money on the line. There are plenty of sites out there that will let you play just for the fun of it, but if you are truly serious about online gambling, you'll come to realize that only when real money is at stake will it be a totally rewarding, adrenaline-pumping casino experience.

Choosing Between Download and Non-Download

Whether you opt for a download site or a non-download site is strictly up to you. If you go download and have Internet Explorer on your PC, choose the option that says "run this program from its current location" rather than "save this program to disc." The process will go much smoother. If you have another browser, such as Netscape, remember to make note of where you save the file you have downloaded and what you named the file so that you'll be able to retrieve it easily without searching aimlessly.

If you choose non-download, you'll want to check out your computer's browser capabilities. Non-download software runs through your browser and will prove only as good as the browser is. If you think you'll be in need of an upgrade, simply check with your browser provider; they'll be more than happy to help you.

As for the technological capabilities of your computer, remember this: If you have anything less than a 56k modem, consider an upgrade. If you have anything less than 128 MB of RAM, consider an upgrade. You will appreciate the speed and ease of play you will enjoy with upgraded equipment. It seems that no sooner have you purchased a computer, and it's already outdated. That's how fast the technology is advancing. In the case of online gambling, however, outdated equipment can make for a very frustrating experience.

In any case you will always enjoy a better playing experience if you have no other active programs or windows on your computer screen while you are logged on to an online casino.

Why Should I Choose to Gamble on the Internet?

The question, however basic it may be, is a good one. If there is a real casino nearby with live dealers, real cards and dice, chips you can feel and cold, hard cash you can buy in and cash out with, why would you choose the virtual reality experience of interacting with a keyboard, mouse pad and video terminal?

I guess the same question could be asked of moviegoers. If there is a big screen theater nearby (and where isn't there?) with comfortable seating, hot movie-style popcorn and other snacks and a great stereo sound, why would you stay home to pop a video cassette in your VCR and watch a movie on your 21-inch or even 50-inch TV screen?

Well, for one thing the clock does not shackle you. When you go out to a movie, you have to adhere to a starting time. In your home, you pop in a cassette any time of the day or night. In a theater, you'll miss some of the movie if you have to use the washroom or head to the concession stand for a snack. At home, you can put the movie on pause when you step away. You must take the time and trouble to walk or drive to a theater and find a parking place. At home you can dress any way you want and plop yourself in your favorite easy chair or spot on the couch. A movie can be pretty expensive for a family. A video can be rented or purchased for a single fee and then viewed by as many people and as often as possible.

As little as 20 years ago, videocassette recorders as a home entertainment option were rare. Today they are so affordable virtually every home has at least one. Yet has the movie industry suffered? On the contrary, movies are more popular than ever. Going to a theater is still the best way to watch a movie, but certainly a cassette, or a DVD, is the next best thing. There are more fans of movies now than at any time in history. Movies are making more money than ever before. The convenience of home movie watching only strengthened the cinema's fan base.

Today mega-theaters with multi-screens are found in cities and suburbs showing every first run and new release available. I can remember the days when a first-run, new release motion picture only played in one theater in any one city. After a few weeks, depending on its popularity, only then would it be distributed to neighborhood theaters. This is very similar to how the casino gaming industry has matured. What once could only be found in Las Vegas can now be found in virtually every region of the country.

Did Las Vegas suffer when gambling opened up in other parts of the country? No way! With the expansion of gambling, and Nevada losing its exclusivity, rather than take away from Vegas, that city became more popular than ever! It was the proliferation of gambling across the land that precipitated the building boom in Las Vegas, the creation of the mega-resorts, and the reinventing of Sin City into a vacation destination for the entire family.

The expansion of gambling created more fans of gambling. Casino gambling has become an acceptable form of entertainment. Casino marketing campaigns have lifted casino gambling out of dark, smoky corridors into the bright lights and electric atmosphere of modern-day casino activity. This expanded fan base was ripe for the casino industry to tap into. It made for a perfect marriage with the burgeoning Internet commerce industry.

Why gamble on the Internet? It is an option that's available to all of us. Sure, there's nothing like the real thing. And as we've already cautioned, there are traps waiting for those who are not wary. There is the convenience factor, the comfort factor, and the gamble-anytime-of-the-day-you-feel-like-it factor.

There are also the dangers of gambling with virtual chips and forgetting about the real value of your money. There is the danger of not having personal contact to create barriers of restraint. When it's you alone against a nameless, faceless, emotionless machine in the confines and safety of your own home, it is easy to become reckless, lose your financial inhibitions and bet (and lose) beyond your means.

Approach Internet gambling with caution and you can't go wrong. Limit yourself, do not play compulsively. When you are not in a live casino environment with fellow players and dealers, it is easy to become the type of player you shouldn't be, often with devastating financial and personal consequences.

Where Are Online Casinos Based and How Are They Regulated?

Gambling on the Internet evolved into a multimillion-dollar business practically overnight. The government of the United States wasn't necessarily caught off guard. The legality of Internet gambling occupies a very gray area of the law to begin with, and that is why, at the present time, all Internet casinos are located outside of the boundaries of the United States of America. Most of the companies that own online casinos do business from the U.S. The catch is that their servers are located in offshore foreign countries.

This is a business phenomenon not unique to Internet casinos. Most major vacation cruise lines that operate out of U.S. ports have their vessels registered in foreign countries. If you've ever taken a cruise, you may have even noticed the ship you were on was flying the flag of its country of origin and not Old Glory. The reason? Cruise-ship operators save millions of dollars in taxes by doing business in this manner.

The foreign countries out of which cruise ships and online casinos are registered are quite content with the setup. Internet gambling companies pay the foreign governments tens of thousands of dollars to obtain a gaming license in these countries, in addition to taxes and other tariffs. The economies of small countries, such as Antigua, Curacao, St. Kitts, Grenada, the Dominican Republic, Gibraltar and the Cook Islands, to name just a sampling, are boosted significantly by hosting online casino businesses. When and if the United States ever sanctions online casino gambling, you better believe the companies that own them as well as the people who patronize them will incur a much bigger tax obligation. Land-based and riverboat casino gambling in the United States as it exists now is heavily taxed, both on a federal as well as a local level.

Just as cruise line operators get around the tax issue by registering their vessels in foreign countries, online casino operators get around the legal issue by registering their sites offshore. Don't think for one minute that Uncle Sam isn't looking into some way to derive more tax revenue from such giant operations.

Because our government doesn't regulate online casinos doesn't necessarily mean that the casinos are corrupt or that they are out to defraud and cheat you. Let's face it, any time you are doing business over the Internet, even under the protection of the government of the United States, you make yourself vulnerable to unscrupulous people.

In light of the fact that online casinos are licensed out of foreign countries, many of which are small island nations with economies that are dwarfed by ours, and systems of government that are not subject to scrutiny, you have to send up more caution flags than usual. After all, if you are defrauded, to whom are you going to complain, the Better Business Bureau? In all cases, even in our own country, the best policy to follow is "let the buyer beware."

Online casinos are in business to make money. Period. They want to attract as many players as they possibly can. The only way to do this is to build a good and honest reputation. If word gets out that a casino reneged on a winner's account, it's going to spread fast. Online casinos, unless it happens to be a shady fly-by-night operation looking for a one-shot killing, have for the most part proved to be safe and honorable.

One telltale sign of a possible nefarious online casino is when it posts a disclaimer along these lines: "For personal rather than professional play." It's their way of telling you that if you are there to turn the tables on them, you may as well hit the road.

The foreign countries out of which the online casinos are based do not necessarily harbor slipshod bureaucracies that allow the casino owners to get away with anything they wish, but never take anything for granted. Many groups must go through a thorough screening process to get a license in the first place. Once they are authorized to conduct business, many of them are required to post funds to prove that they can ante up.

The best advice is to never let your guard down. The opportunity is ripe for cheats. Some of the countries out of which the online casinos are based lack laws and legislation to protect people from gambling fraud.

Another caveat to remember is that many so-called online casino regulator and watchdog groups and agencies are not objective bodies at all, but in reality subjective bodies with ties, direct or indirect, to online casino owners and operators. Be very careful of the opinions expressed by such groups and the recommendations that they make. They could, after all, turn out to be valid, but the opinions are sometimes not based on fact but rather on bias. Your own power of investigation and good old-fashioned common sense are necessary companions to any advice you seek.

Take the Interactive Gaming Council (IGC) for an example. It awards "Seal of Approval" designation to casinos it deems reputable and honest, but the fact is the IGC is a trade organization made up of 80 companies around the world that are actively involved in the Internet gaming industry. These include operators of Internet gaming sites. The IGC is no doubt looking out to police its own best interests to a certain extent, which filters down to being an advantage to players. But you must keep in mind that a lot of the opinions it expresses may not be totally unbiased or objective as those of a totally independent watchdog group would be.

On the surface of things, the IGC does hold approved sites to a higher standard. They insist on such things as accountability to consumers, privacy and data protection, truth in advertising, banking and transaction processing, among other protections. In the absence of government regulation, the IGC could be an important first step and better than nothing when it comes to seeking out an honest site.

Technical Systems Testing, based in Melbourne, Victoria, in Australia, evaluates gaming systems, including Internet casinos. But unless the government of the country in which the Internet casino is based also insists on regulatory controls to ensure that the interests of the public are protected, it really is a paper tiger. Unless an online game is tested and regulated by an independent agency as well as government authorities, there is no 100 percent guarantee the game is honest.

If you are concerned about personal information that you may transmit online to Internet casinos, such as name, address, credit card numbers, etc., you must understand that these are similar causes for concern anytime you send that same information online to a company licensed outside of the United States. There are dangers inherent no matter what.

Reputable online casinos make every effort to keep any personal information that you may send to them secure. More often than not, it is guaranteed under the licensing agreements. Furthermore, most use secure servers for all transactions, and none of the information is available online, which puts a stop to hackers and others looking to manipulate the Internet to their own devices.

Internet casinos want to attract business; they also want to attract big business and big bettors. They know that people who are willing to bet a lot of money are supersensitive about personal information regarding their avocation. If they compromise this trust, they'll lose the very clientele they are seeking.

Getting Started

With the literally hundreds of online gaming sites that are available, and that number growing every day, it is virtually impossible to recommend one site over another. Some come and go. Others have staying power. Some are more sophisticated in terms of animation, sound and graphics, some have a bigger variety of games, particularly in the slots and video poker categories. Some are pretty much meat and potatoes gambling, others are a gourmet gambler's delight. In a majority of respects, they are all pretty much the same. Certainly, there are some very bad ones that should be avoided, especially since there are so many better ones from which to choose.

You certainly cannot go by the advertising some of them put out in various publications and online. They're all going to say they are the best, they are all going to offer the best sign-on bonuses and they are going to have the best games and best payouts. But the truth of the matter is they all don't. The best way to go about it is to find out for yourself. Surf the net by logging onto a search engine using the category online casinos or online gambling. Check out as many sites as possible to see the variations, the deposit requirements, minimum bets, bonuses, games available and the download time, if any.

Don't make any hasty decisions. Remember that gambling on the Internet is a luxury, not a necessity. If possible, find sites that will allow you to practice by playing for fun. There are a number of such sites available. You will not only get a feel for the particular site, you will also get some experience using the site without risking anything. Find out as much as you possibly can about any online casino that interests you. Don't be fooled or influenced by the subjective information that is supplied on site. By its very nature it'll be totally biased. Seek out as much objective information as possible.

When you find an online casino you like and are comfortable with, you will be required to sign up on an online form if you want to establish an account and play for real money. The information they will require of you may vary. For all practical purposes, you will be anonymous, an account number with a personal password that allows you to log onto the online casino. Other sites might require your name and address.

Now the most important component of your decision to sign up with an online casino is depositing money into your personal account. It's serious business, to be sure. Any time you make the decision to transfer funds from one account to another, or make a verbal or online transaction using your credit card, there is some risk involved. There have been numerous instances of credit card fraud within the confines of the United States.

You won't be able to play unless money has been verifiably deposited in your account. Among the options available are credit cards, money orders, cashier's checks, Western Union and Moneygram. Remember that there are transaction fees connected with this practice, so always be aware up front how much it's costing you. Credit card transactions over the Internet are the quickest and most cost efficient. You're at the mercy of the mail with some of the other methods. As for personal checks, you'll have to wait for the instrument to clear, even if you have check cashing approval from the online casino with which you're doing business. It is the least recommended means of deposit.

If you use your credit card, gratification is almost instantaneous. Approval can take a matter of minutes and you'll be ready to play. The most efficient online casinos will credit whatever card you choose to use within several days of cashing out. There are minimum deposit requirements, which vary in amount, but are usually around the $25 to $50 level.

The popularity of using credit cards to establish online gambling accounts has also spawned abuse on the part of gamblers who, in isolated cases, have refused to pay the debts that they have incurred. Credit card companies and the banks that issue the cards, therefore, have begun to impose restrictions on the use of their cards for online gambling purposes.

Most casino software requires 30 minutes to download on the average home computer. Once it's there, stored on your computer's hard drive, you won't have to worry about downloading it again. The down side is you won't be able to play unless you are working with that particular computer.

If you go the JAVA route (casinos which require no download), you may sacrifice graphics and sound quality, but you will also be able to play from any computer by logging on with your account number and password.

Finally, start up your account with the minimum amount that is required. Test the waters to see if you like the conditions, if the games seem to be giving you a fair shake and it's the kind of experience you bargained for. Only after you confirm this should you even think about beefing up your account.

Also, check for prompt, accurate action when it comes to your account. When online casinos dillydally about getting your money to you, there is definite cause for concern. They wouldn't let you play without a confirmed transfer of your funds to them. Why should you hold them to any less a standard?

Of course, if you want to assure accurate handling of your account, always keep your own personal records of how much you have gambled, what your win/loss ledger looks like and what the status of your account really is. Hold the online casino to this figure precisely! At this time, you should also be on the lookout for veiled fees and related charges.

Are Online Casinos on the Level?

Any Internet casino worth its salt is going to give gamblers a fair shake. They want to make playing online as close to being in a live casino as possible. With the hundreds of online sites out there, it is imperative that you seek the ones that make their product as attractive as live casinos. Pay particular attention to payback percentages for slot machines, payback tables for video poker machines, odds and rules for table games and the variety of gambling options in each category that the site makes available.

Even though there is no internal government regulation of online casino gambling within the United States, it's a fact that many countries in which the online casinos are licensed require the owners to have their computer programs checked for authenticity, accuracy and reliability. Is this accuracy check for real or is it just a sham? In isolated instances it can be just a cover-up to lull gamblers into a false sense of trust. That's the price to be paid for gambling in unregulated cyberspace.

The online gambling industry in its present form offers no real, ironclad guarantees in all instances that the games are honest, that prompt and accurate payment of winnings will be made, that users are not breaking some law or that credit card numbers will not be misused in some way.

One very big advantage that online gambling has over its live counterpart: shopping around for the best games. In real casinos, players are at the mercy of the locality in which they live. You may like to play $5.00 minimum hand blackjack or like to take advantage of 20-times odds at the craps table, but unless those games are available at a casino near you, you're out of luck. Thanks to online gambling, you don't need to travel hundreds of miles or even buy an airline ticket to find the best games. Shopping is right at your fingertips on the Internet.

With this in mind, it is well worth the investment in time and effort to seek out the best odds and payback percentages. The odds in blackjack will, of course, be the same online as in a live casino. But will the rules always be the same? Better check it out. Does the dealer hit or stand on soft 17s? Can you double down after splitting?

There are also slight rule variations to look for in craps, such as the amount of free odds you can take, the bonus payoffs on snake-eyes (2) and midnight (12) in the field, if the one-roll proposition bets pay *for* one (as in 3 for 1 which equals a win of two chips plus your original bet = 3 chips returned) or the more player-friendly *to* one (as in 3 to 1 which means you win three chips and your original bet = 4 chips returned). Most of the other table games such as baccarat, variations of poker and roulette, are all very similar in that the odds are standard and rule variations at a minimum.

Slot machines and video poker are another story. The only fact about slot machines that customers are made aware of when they play them in a live casino is the average theoretical payout of the aggregate machines in the house. The higher the percentage return to customers the better, even though the payback percentages of individual machines are usually an unknown. My advice is to insist on playing the online casinos that reveal what its slot payback percentage really is. If such a figure is unavailable, avoid playing there because there are so many others available that will give you that information.

As for video poker, be sure to investigate the posted paytables for the best games, just as all shrewd video poker players should do when they visit a live casino. Unlike slot machines, which have payout percentages based on computer programs installed by the manufacturer, video poker winning and losing is based on pure mathematical probability of the various combinations in a 52-card or 53-card (one joker) deck. The great equalizer for the casino is the paytables, which are available for all to see and interpret. The better the paytable, the better the game for the player and the higher percentage return based on expert play.

Game Analysis: Slot Machines

The name of the game when it comes to slot machine play is variety. The bigger the variety of games the better. You wouldn't want to go to a real casino and have only one or two slot machine game formats from which to choose; online gambling should be no different. A site with a few obligatory choices gives you the opportunity to play, all right, but it certainly isn't what playing in a casino is all about. Slot machine play means you have an entire casino floor from which to pick and choose. What denomination? Do you like progressives? Single line? Multi-line? Multiple coin?

The slot machines located in today's live casinos, particularly the video versions, put a premium on interaction and entertainment. You don't want to go to an online casino and get stuck playing a boring, one-dimensional game just for the sake of playing. Slot machine play has evolved into a thoroughly entertaining experience. Don't go back in time by playing online if the games are not to your liking.

Curiously, some of the cautions inherent in playing slot machines online also exist in land-based casinos. Every slot machine's computer program houses a unique digital signature. In the real world, if a casino's machines are not linked to a central monitoring system, the only way to check the integrity of a machine is to physically open it up and examine the computer chip. With a central monitoring system, it can be examined easily and electronically from a remote location.

Don't frown when you hear there is no central monitoring system required for online casino slots. In Nevada, which has more slot machines than any other state, central monitoring is not required. But in Colorado, a much smaller gaming jurisdiction, it is required. All of the electronic gaming devices in use in Australia are online to a central monitoring system. Central monitoring of slots makes it possible to check the machine's integrity at any time, such as when it is turned on, when a jackpot is won, or randomly as a fail-safe testing system.

This doesn't imply there is corruption, but sometimes machines are faulty. Much can be done to ensure the integrity of the machines and thereby satisfy the doubts of the gambling public.

If you do find a site you like, be sure to make a thorough analysis of the games. Is payback percentage posted? If not, you may be trapped into playing a machine with payoff expectations far below what you may find in a live casino. Are the graphics appealing, the animation entertaining and the sound effects what you were looking for? If not, don't stick around.

A preferable online site will have a variety of games that includes individual machines as well as progressives. As with play in any casino, if you choose a progressive, don't

play with less than maximum coin. If you do, you'll be totally defeating the purpose of choosing that particular game
format. Also, be aware of the pay tables just as you would in
any casino. Are the payoffs proportional to the number of
coins played, or will you incur a major jackpot penalty for less
than maximum coins played?

Some online casinos make slots very player friendly,
offering perks that include an icon to check the size of the various progressive jackpots that are available.

There are generally slot games to fit every budget,
including nickel, quarter, dollar and five-dollar versions. If a
site does not give you this flexibility, don't bet beyond your
means or budget. Just check out another casino.

One caution sign for online casino players is to be sure
to check that the denomination you desire to play is, in fact,
the denomination you are playing. If you are activating a
three-coin dollar game instead of the three-coin quarter game
you wanted, you'll be spending $3 a spin instead of the 75
cents that you budgeted. Don't be in a hurry. If you go to
another game, some online casino default settings will bring
you back to the dollar setting instead of the quarter setting
that you were in. Stay alert.

The same pitfalls that wait for slot players in live casinos exist in online casinos. The price that you pay for playing
casino games (the dreaded house advantage) can hit you particularly hard at slots primarily because of the speed at which
you can play. Slow down. If you go into a game post haste
and start activating a play every few seconds or so, the edge,
no matter how small it may be, is going to eat you alive.

Game Analysis: Video Poker

What makes video poker such an appealing game in
live casinos is not always the case when playing online. Allow
me to explain: The edge that video poker players enjoy over

traditional slot players is that they can determine precisely what the percentage return of a machine is based on the paytable. Since video poker is based on the random shuffling of 52 or 53 cards, an analysis of the paytable can reveal just what percentage of all the money played in a machine is returned to the player. Unfortunately, slot players are not privy to this information since they don't know the odds of any given symbol hitting.

In video poker, the factor that distinguishes one game from another, the good games from the bad games, are the paytables, which are in full view for everyone to see (at least they should be). First and most important, if you don't see the video-poker game's paytable online, don't play. It's that simple. When you do see the paytable, examine it carefully before you even think about playing. The information contained in it is so critical to your play that you cannot ignore it or take it lightly.

It is an unfortunate generalization when playing video poker on an online casino that the game is nowhere near as advantageous for the player as it is in a real casino. Many of the games with which you are familiar are altered to favor the house much more when playing online. Even though a version of the popular Jacks or Better may appear to offer full pay (that is 9/6 for the full house and flush), the paytable may be weaker in other premium hands such as four-of-a-kind and straight flush, which will reduce the overall return significantly.

Some of the reductions can be quite dramatic. Even on the most popular versions of video poker, which offer paybacks very close to one hundred percent in most real casinos, online versions can dip into the low nineties if there is enough pay table manipulation. That's why you have to be wary, even if an online casino advertises a game as 9/6 Jacks or Better. It certainly may reflect correct returns for the full house and flush, but payoffs for higher hands are liable to be slashed.

Variety of games varies, but if you are given a variety of low paying games, what's the difference? Online video poker is one game that requires serious players to shop around very carefully. The game can be so different from its real casino cousin that in many cases it isn't even worth playing. The price you pay is simply too great.

Most online casinos offer the whole gamut of denominations ranging from a nickel to five dollars. You must check the default setting when switching from game to game. If you're playing a Jacks or Better game and jump over to Deuces Wild, the default may go back to one dollar. If you were playing quarters, you could be in for a shock after a hand or two on the new game.

Game Analysis: Craps

The game of casino craps can be as simple or as complicated to play as you wish. It has a wider variety of bets than any casino game, and the more, the merrier. The more selection of bets, the more advantageous the play. With this in mind, some versions of online craps for the serious player can leave a lot to be desired. If you want to be shackled by limited wagering opportunities, online craps can be a poor substitute for its real green-felt counterpart.

There are no paytables for online casinos to fool around with in craps. The mathematics of the game is a constant, with the exception of field bets and proposition bets. In the field, for example, doubling the payoff for snake eyes and boxcars makes the field wager somewhat more acceptable. But if a casino triples the odds on one of the numbers, it can be much more attractive from an odds standpoint.

Taking advantage of the best odds in craps make pass and don't pass, come and don't come and place bets on the numbers six and eight essential to have. Another serious consideration is free odds. A casino must offer double odds or better if you want to make it a game worth playing. If there are only single odds, just close it down and look for a better game.

You must be on guard for house rules, too. If an online casino requires you to bet the line in order to make other bets, this is a negative when it comes to enjoying the freedom the real version of the game offers.

Appealing graphics and animation are at a premium when playing craps on line. It's just a matter of shopping around and not jumping into the very first game you find.

Game Analysis: Blackjack

Whereas online craps can hold you hostage with limited wagering opportunities, online blackjack can hold you hostage with rules. Rules vary widely from house to house in real casinos. Can you imagine what it is like online? How many decks are in play? Can you double down on any two cards? Can you double after splits? Does the dealer hit soft 17? How many times can you resplit pairs? Is insurance available? How about surrender? Every edge an online casino takes on the rules is an edge taken away from the players, making the game less advantageous to play.

There are also some weird aspects of online blackjack play that you won't encounter in most flesh and blood casinos. For example, if you're playing on felt, most casinos will allow you to take only one card on each of your split aces. There are some online casinos that will allow you to take more than one card on split aces. That's a definite advantage for the player. Or how about casinos that do not require their dealers to check for a blackjack with a 10-value up card? If you've got a split or a double down on the layout and the dealer has an ace in the hole for a blackjack, most casinos won't take both of your bets but some online casinos do. It's just a matter of checking the rules.

There are some real traps to avoid. In a live casino, if
you are dealt a blackjack and the dealer has an ace showing,
you have the option of taking even money. If the dealer winds
up with a blackjack, your hand will be a push. There have
been online examples of the house winning if both the dealer
and the player have blackjack. Incredible! This moves up the
house edge quite significantly and is a game option to be
avoided at all costs.

Never, ever accept online blackjack play for rules that
you would not accept in a real casino. After all, if you are a
blackjack aficionado and enjoy taking every edge you can,
playing online is a poor substitute for the real thing to begin
with, because most online casinos shuffle up after every
hand, making counting techniques useless.

There are exceptions. Some of the bigger online casinos
offer as many as six variations of blackjack, including a single-deck game, a six-deck game and a Spanish 21 game. On
occasion you'll come across a multi-deck game in which the
cards are not shuffled after every hand.

Game Analysis: Roulette

Just as in real casinos, the online version of roulette is
pretty much standard with one very notable exception. As in
the real world, most casinos offer the American version of the
game, or the wheel with a zero and a double zero. This gives
the house a 5.26 percent advantage. There are some cyberspace roulette havens which have the European version, or
the wheel with a single zero, which slashes the casino's edge
to 2.70 percent. That is the game to look for.

Some sites that have single-zero roulette will also make
the "la partage" rule available. Under this system, if you have
a wager on one of the even money propositions (black/red,
odd/even, high/low) and the ball lands on zero, you only

lose half your bet which cuts the house edge even further, to 1.35 percent.

There are isolated instances of roulette hybrids. One such game I encountered was called Wild American with a *zero percent* house edge! When you do come across them, always investigate before jumping in with your funds. Online casinos are not in business to give money away. They are in business to take your money. Beware of any offer that seems too good to be true.

Good graphics and animation can make playing roulette on some online casinos better than others. The more realistic, the better, in light of the fact roulette is a fairly slow-paced game that allows for a little relaxation as well as gambling enjoyment. Some online casinos will offer a feature that keeps track of the numbers that have been hit, but what's the use when you're not dealing with a real wheel made of metal and wood, and furthermore, a human dealer who can be subject to idiosyncrasies, conscious or unconscious? [For a complete rundown on how to take advantage of the casino version of roulette, get Christopher Pawlicki's *Get the Edge at Roulette: How to Predict Where the Ball Will Land!* Bonus Books.]

Don't sell this form of online roulette record keeping short. Just as in blackjack, where cards are dealt according to random numbers generated by a random number generator (RNG), numbers in roulette are also generated by the RNG, which can be a special circuit or actually a part of the particular computer software you're dealing with.

Other Games and Bonus Offers

A good general rule of thumb for online bettors to subscribe to is this: Avoid playing games online that you would avoid playing in the real world. If you walk past the keno area in live casinos, if you wouldn't be caught dead playing War or Red Dog, if you don't play BINGO, if you don't purchase scratch-off instant lottery tickets, by all means don't do it online! The odds are just as bad in cyberspace as they are in real space.

As for games such as Caribbean Poker, Let It Ride, Three Card Poker and to a lesser extent, Baccarat and Spanish 21, be careful that you are not tricked into playing a hybrid version with a similar-sounding name but with entirely different rules and house edges.

As is the case with real life casinos, do not allow bonuses to dictate where you play or how you play on an online casino. As the old saying goes, "there is no such thing as a free lunch." Online casinos do not offer bonuses and perks because they're nice guys. They make those offers because they want your business and they want your business to ultimately pay for what you are seemingly getting from them for nothing.

Always be sure to read the fine print about whatever bonuses are offered. There are many clauses and conditions. If it was that easy, all you'd have to do to make money on Internet casinos would be to jump around signing up and collecting bonuses. There is often a minimum deposit for a required length of time and an amount of play that is expected of you. There are gambling thresholds set that the casino requires you to meet before you become eligible to receive the bonus. Use caution when being lured by sign-on and playing bonuses.

Helpful Online Casino Information

As a general rule of thumb, the longer an online casino has been up and running the better. It just makes sense. The obvious staying power is proof that it's not a fly-by-night operation looking to make a few quick scams and then absconding with the funds. Longevity of several years is an eternity as far as online casinos are concerned. The site obviously has customer loyalty and customers keep coming back because they keep getting paid. In short, it's an honest operation that in all likelihood gives players a good gamble.

The more sophisticated a site is as far as visuals are concerned and the more variety of games and number of games, the better the site is. Smaller sites with little variety and limited games just don't give you the proper opportunity to shop around. It's like going to a one-dimensional clothing store as opposed to browsing through a department store.

If you are playing an online casino where you lose the connection, or where play is slow and cumbersome, it's time to look around for something bigger and better. Why not take advantage of the variety and number of online casinos? As I have already established, Internet casino gambling makes hundreds of casinos available to you literally at your fingertips. Traveling through cyberspace does have its privileges!

When shopping around for an online casino, look for ones that have a support number or e-mail address to contact, preferably open 24 hours a day. Give a call to test the services that are available and the quality of the service. When you play online you want to know that you can reach somebody with a question should anything go wrong. The bigger and better sites are doing this now. You also want to know what kind of safeguards they provide if you lose the connection during the middle of play.

A key fact you'll want to know right off the bat about an online casino is the site's software provider. Some of the best and most reliable include Starnet, Gambling Software.com, Microgaming, Unified Gaming, Real Time Gaming, Boss Media and Cryptologic. I will delve into specifics about these software providers later in the book.

A Starnet-powered online casino, for example, runs its operation through a subsidiary company called Electronic Financial Services International, Inc. They ensure credit card security through the use of proprietary encoding and processing technology. Starnet-powered online casinos also ensure players' personal information will not be shared with a third party. Given the number of Starnet-powered casinos that are available, strength in numbers is a prime factor when speculating about an online operation's integrity.

Horse Racing Is in a Class by Itself

Long before the popularity of casino gambling as a recreational and leisure-time activity spread across the country, before there were state-run lotteries and Internet gambling, before college and pro sports dominated office-run betting pools, horse racing reigned as the entertainment of choice for people with an inclination to place a bet.

Horse racing was covered as a major sport on a daily basis. The results of the traditional Daily Double were printed on the front page of the nation's evening newspapers. The first late morning edition of the paper was called the turf edition because it contained the late scratches from tracks around the country.

Betting on horse races on site was legal in all states with pari-mutuel wagering legislation, but even kids back in horse racing's hey day knew that all book makers didn't work in binderies. Friendly, neighborhood bookies could be found at corner newsstands, bars and the work place.

Horse racing, particularly thoroughbred horse racing, was a fact of life in America. It enjoyed a reputation as the nation's No. 1 spectator sport for decades. Racetrack grandstands in major cities were filled to capacity on weekends and holidays.

So what happened? Competition for America's entertainment dollar, that's what! State lotteries, casinos, the proliferation of motor sports, in-home entertainment outlets such as VCRs and DVDs and the expansion of other sports and the duration of their seasons have all helped to push horse racing out of the limelight.

In some respects, horse racing has also been forced to play second fiddle to sports betting. Despite the fact that wagering on the outcome of athletic events is illegal in every state except Nevada, newspapers everywhere are loaded with odds tables, point spreads and other wagering information pertaining to football, basketball, baseball and other sports. The majority of the newspapers' gamblers are not placing their bets at the sports books of Las Vegas but with their local bookies.

How about pro football season? Can you imagine the number of office pools that go on from week to week, not to mention fantasy leagues? How about March Madness in college basketball? Some papers devote full pages to the playoff grid for the high profile NCAA tournament, the majority of which wind up taped to office walls for the betting pools.

The fact of the matter is this: Horse racing is legal in many states, yet it is treated like a redheaded step child as far as the electronic and print media are concerned. With the noteworthy exceptions of the Triple Crown races in the spring and the Breeders' Cup races in the fall, racing gets little big league coverage.

Some of horse racing's fall from public grace is its own fault. When television coverage of the other major sports began, the moguls of racing felt they would be "giving their product away" by exposing it on the tube. A generation of youngsters grew up with baseball as prime TV viewing, while horse racing was left to live audiences of adults.

The sport deserves much better. In addition to being exciting, it offers one of the very best wagering opportunities a bettor can find anywhere. Here are just three reasons why:

1. Because horse racing is first and foremost a sport, there is a definite skill factor involved when it comes to plac-

ing a wager. Sure, luck plays a role, but there is enough cerebral input to make it a worthwhile enterprise for any thinking, enterprising speculator who takes his gambling seriously.

2. In horse racing, you are not wagering against the house as you do in a casino. You are wagering against your fellow bettors. It's called pari-mutuel (a French derivation for "wagering among ourselves"). The host track extracts a percentage of the dollars that are bet and the remainder is distributed to the players in the form of winnings. The racetrack gets the same cut regardless if a favorite or a long-shot wins the race.

3. The takeout in horse racing is quite manageable; especially when you consider the heavy skill factor which players can take advantage of. Win, place and show wagering takeout runs around 17 percent. Takeout on exotic bets, such as Quinellas, Perfectas, and Trifectas, ranges from 20 to 25 percent. Not bad when you consider most state lotteries extract 50 percent of every dollar wagered.

Horse racing can also be a much more affordable leisure-time activity than going to a casino. It's possible to walk into a race track with a twenty-dollar bill in your pocket, wager a couple of dollars on every race, and have a ball for several hours. Take that same double sawbuck to a casino, step up to a cold slot machine, and it'll disappear in no time flat.

As with all forms of gambling, the seriousness with which you approach the sport of horse racing is directly proportional to the long-term success you are liable to enjoy. This doesn't take into account the sheer fun of it. It also doesn't mean you can't win an occasional bet on a lucky number, a grandchild's name, a favorite color or simply because you just like the way the horse looks.

For the uninitiated, a day at the races can be one of the most pleasant events you'll ever experience. The majesty of the animals themselves, the color and pageantry that is part of the sport and the athletic prowess required of the jockeys, all add up to a day out of doors that cannot be beat.

The Evolution of Handicapping

If you play the horses (a most unflattering phrase I have never been overly fond of), there has never been a better time to be alive than today. There is more information, more sources from which to obtain that information easily, efficiently and inexpensively, and more opportunities to take advantage of skilled, intelligent, and rational methods to select winners than at any other time in the colorful history of thoroughbred horse racing.

The sport itself is steeped in tradition, a constant in a sea of change that has rocked other sports to their very foundations. The very premise of thoroughbred racing is simple: To run as fast as you can for as long as you can. Track surfaces and the equipment used to maintain them have changed, but for the most part little has changed in the sport for almost a century.

Whereas the fastest recorded times in other sports have plummeted through the years, particularly the sport of harness racing in which breeding and equipment have made a tremendous positive impact on performance, the fastest times for the various distances in thoroughbred racing have not seen dramatic changes. Dr. Fager's world record for a mile of 1:32 1/5 set in 1968 at Chicago's Arlington Park stood for 29 years. His 7-furlongs track record of 1:20 1/5 set the same year at Aqueduct Race Track in New York stood for 30 years.

Wagering on the outcome of horse races goes back centuries. The thoroughbred racehorse, blessed with a competitive nature, speed and endurance, was a most natural focal point for this pursuit. Organized racing meetings and the formation of corporate racing enterprises known as jockey clubs began in earnest in post–Civil War America.

Betting on horse races became the domain of the bookmakers, private entrepreneurs who competed against one another for betting dollars. Pari-mutuels, a system by which tracks take and hold the bets and distribute money to the winners in exchange for a percentage of the total money wagered, put the bookmakers out of business in post–World War I America.

The legendary horseplayer George "Pittsburgh Phil" Smith is credited with being the father of the scientific method as it applies to picking the winners of horse races. Plying his trade in the late 1880s and early 1900s, an era when past performance data and other information was practically nonexistent, Smith kept his own journals and records in notebook form. His handicapping prowess made him a wealthy man and a famous one, even outside of horse racing circles.

It was said that Smith's success was not so much the result of his methods but rather the manner in which he applied them to betting. It was true then and it is true now; the merit of any gambling system lies not in its theory but in its practical application. Here is where a gambler's individual personality comes into play. In other words, there is a huge difference between picking winners and winning money.

Pittsburgh Phil died in 1905 at the age of 43. Three years later an interview that had been conducted with him was published in book form and titled *Racing Maxims & Methods of Pittsburgh Phil*. Among the topics covered are the element of time, the importance of class and weight, the proper treatment of horses, drugs and their effect on horses and an unprecedented study of weight and how it affects time.

A testimonial to the timeless nature of the sport is the fact that no less an authority than Howard Schwartz, marketing director for the renowned Gambler's Book Shop in Las Vegas since 1979, lists Pittsburgh Phil's book among the best/most significant books ever written for the player or about the gambling industry.

Schwartz, whose Gambler's Book Club is widely recognized as having the most comprehensive selection of books on gambling in the world, defines best in terms of its "relationship to the actual impact each book has had on developing or encouraging players." *Racing Maxims & Methods of Pittsburgh Phil*, originally published in 1908 and last reprinted in 1994, is still available. States Schwartz: "It stimulated, guided and advised untold millions of horse players for generations throughout the 20th Century with its common-sense approach. This book guided many a first-time horse player to the track to test theories for the first time. Much of what Phil said 100 years ago has been refined by others and applies even today."

That is truly incredible. Can you imagine a book written 100 years ago about virtually any other sport still having validity today? If the foundation of the art of handicapping is that timeless and unwavering, it only makes sense that the multitude of information and data that's available now only enhances the prospects of success for any individual willing to devote the time and energy to applying them.

It has been said that a baseball box score as it is printed in daily newspapers contains more information column inch for column inch than any other printed matter. I would venture to say that an individual racehorse's past performance record or a chart of a thoroughbred horse race contains as much information or possibly more. Past performances and charts in one form or another have been kept since the mid 1800s. The quality of information and the degree of accuracy have improved dramatically, especially during the last decade.

If you were to study the past performance charts of horses as they were printed as short a time ago as the late 1960s and compare them to how they look today, you'd be amazed. There were no fractional running times, no career records, no lifetime records of performance on turf (grass) courses, just to name a few. If an individual kept his or her own records of horses, it was possible to gain a significant edge over those who didn't.

Today, there is so much information available in past performances about a horse's racing career, very little is left to the individual handicapper to uncover. Add to that the availability of the Internet, videotape libraries of races, computer databases and so much more, today is truly a horseplayer's dream. If Pittsburgh Phil weren't already there, he'd certainly be in heaven if he were alive today.

Bringing the Sport into the 21st Century

If the sport of thoroughbred racing itself hasn't changed much, the way it is packaged and presented certainly has. The most significant and dramatic reasons for this are as follows:

1. Extended racing seasons across the country. This ended the practice of stables following circuits and paved the way for the creation of a more provincial brand of sport, one in which fewer numbers of horsemen traveled to other tracks. Horse colonies tended to stagnate, and, most important, handicappers lost one of their most valuable angles: tabbing horses for courses.

2. Competition from other sports and alternative gambling venues. Thoroughbred racing began to lose its presence in the daily paper as other sports went through dramatic growth spurts. Professional sports leagues expanded, seasons were extended and motor sports began to spread to all parts of the country. What's more, state lotteries began to pop up all over the country, followed by the explosion of casino gambling in the 90s.

3. Full-card simulcasting of races and off-track betting. This, more than anything else, forever changed the sport. Once upon a time, you had to go to the track to watch and bet on the races, and the track you were at was the only track on whose races you could bet, legally. This was the foundation of a strong local racing product and thriving circuits. Then along came state legislation to open up off-track betting networks which resulted in the birth of a new generation of racing fans whose only connection with the sport was a betting machine and a TV screen. Finally, additional legislation legalized full-card simulcasting whereby fans can watch and bet on races from other tracks around the country. It made every race track a mini-version of a Las Vegas sports book.

4. Consolidation of race tracks. Full-card simulcasting made the world of racing much smaller and created a vision into the future in which smaller tracks and lesser markets would wither and die. Opening up the opportunity to watch and wager on the very best races and horses to bettors all around the country proved too big a temptation, resulting in an inordinate amount of wagering dollars being bet on out-of-state products. Simulcasting revenues began to escalate, creating a climate for the corporate takeover of tracks and the formation of umbrella racing operations seeking a lock on a major share of simulcasting revenues the year 'round.

The landscape of thoroughbred racing is being altered dramatically because of this phenomenon. Canadian industrialist Frank Stronach and Churchill Downs, Inc. have emerged as the major players coast-to-coast by making key acquisitions in many of the major markets, drawing the battle lines for grabbing major shares of the simulcast market and at the same time setting the stage for the sport's future.

If betting online and via simulcast is indeed the future of the sport at the expense of attending the races live and in person, we could very well be looking at a time in the not too distant future when a handful of major tracks operating year round will become what thoroughbred racing is all about.

5. Betting on horse races over the Internet. In a very short period of time, horse bettors have been taken from watching live thoroughbred racing on track, to watching closed-circuit television signals of the sport in off-track parlors, to watching and betting from the comfort of their own homes via an Internet connection and a lap top computer. This has opened up a new era in betting on races, and is a peek into the future on the destiny of horse racing.

A Professional's Perspective

Betting on horse races over the Internet is the ultimate in convenience, especially for handicappers who take the sport seriously. It has enabled students of the game, who were previously only able to attend the races on weekends, to keep in regular touch with the sport and to accumulate the kind of information that's possible only when you are able to watch every race, every day.

Just ask professional handicapper David Gutfreund, well known in handicapping circles nationwide. He is one of a select group of individuals who makes his living handicapping the races and by entering handicapping tournaments that are held at racetracks across the country and sponsored by casinos. Gutfreund brings handicapping to a new level by approaching it in much the same way as an investor looks at the stock market, or a speculator looks at commodities.

When you get right down to it, handicapping horses and investing in stocks and commodities are very similar, yet the pursuits project very different impressions. Just ask Gutfreund: "When I tell people what I do, most of the time they react very negatively. Yet I put just as much work and research into selecting horses as an investor does selecting a stock or speculating on futures. A guy walks down the street with a *Daily Racing Form* under his arm and people say he's a bum. A guy walks down the street with a *Wall Street Journal* under his arm and he's looked upon with respect. It doesn't figure."

Much of thoroughbred racing's unsavory image is the result of Hollywood and theatrical stereotyping. Through the years horse racing has been portrayed over and over again as corrupt. Horse players invariably are portrayed as fast-talking con men with checkered coats, or down-on-their-luck dreamers with tattered trousers and holes in their shoes.

It's really very unfair. Handicapping the races is a cerebral enterprise involving research of past performance, keen powers of observation and the art known as reading between the lines when it comes to digesting statistical information and making it work for future gain. Sound like stock and commodity trading? You bet it does.

Gutfreund's talent as a handicapper was tapped early on by Youbet.com, the first mass-marketed Internet company specializing in online horse racing and wagering at tracks around the country. By setting up a wagering account and installing prescribed software in your PC, Youbet.com made going to the track as easy as sitting in your easy chair at home. Later on I'll expand on the services provided by Youbet.com.

Youbet.com enlisted the services of experts across the country to be the on-track eyes and ears of account holders. By posting up-to-the-minute information and making expert observations as only a trained and experienced eye can do, Gutfreund made invaluable input available to account holders in plenty of time for them to make their wagers. In many respects, the service is better than being there.

By enrolling with the online horse racing and wagering service, you acquire much more than the capability to wager legally on races from tracks around the country. In addition to the information you yourself are able to download and digest, the company's expert, on-track observer can convey information to bettors electronically as the information is received.

For example, how is the horse warming up? An expert who is live on scene for every race, every day, picks up valuable information about each horse's individual patterns and characteristics. Unless you are able to be at the track every day, and have the knowledge and wherewithal to make such cogent, bet-altering observations, you are in the dark. Online horse-race betting can be the answer.

What about track bias? Veteran horseplayers know it not only changes from day to day, it can change from race to race. Weather, temperature, track harrowing, even the day of the week, can have effects on the depth of the racing surface. At times there is a decided path that astute jockeys can pick up on to gain the kind of edge that makes the difference between winning and losing. After all, noses decide races, which amounts to a minute fraction of a second when time is taken into account. An on-track observer will not only be able to fill you in on changes in track bias; you will have the services of an expert who is able to pick up on the biases and send the information to you the instant it becomes available.

Many other kinds of information can also be sent, such as how a horse appears physically after a race and how that could possibly affect his performance the next time he runs. You'll be able to find out about horses who got into trouble during a race, were stopped behind a tiring opponent, were forced to alter course, were victims of poor judgment on behalf of the rider and which horses did not like the running surface that day.

There are little things such as how a horse warms up prior to the race. Does he appear alert and eager to run? Or is he a little stiff, possibly showing signs of being sore? Are there any visible differences from the last time he appeared on track? What if the horse is fractious and throws his rider in the post parade or during the warm-ups? Unless you are there, you cannot be aware of such vital bet-altering information. If you are forced to bet in advance, your investment is imprisoned. Taking advantage of an online full-service horse racing and wagering company such as Youbet.com opens the window of opportunity for you to know this information the instant it happens.

What an advantage online wagering makes to horseplayers! When betting on out-of-state races was made possible through simulcast-wagering legislation, horseplayers acquired the ability to take their knowledge to broader horizons, rather than being prisoners of the track that was close to home. It would be similar to a stock market observer being able to track stocks only in his city. Simulcast wagering brought horse playing to the big board, a New York Stock Exchange impact on the sport and its followers.

Now online wagering has taken big board horse betting to a bold new horizon by not only allowing players to bet on races from around the country, but to do it with the most sensory and statistical information available. What's more, horseplayers have gained the freedom to conduct their business from the privacy of their homes, a luxury previously reserved only for stock market investors who'd place a call to their broker from their kitchen wall phone.

Unlike online casinos, which skirt the bounds of legality by being licensed out of foreign countries, a service such as Youbet.com is a legal online service operated within the boundaries of the United States of America. The money taken from players' individual accounts is sent to the tracks via a hub location, in the case of Youbet.com, Ladbroke in Pennsylvania. Youbet.com makes contractual agreements with race tracks to enlist their races as part of the service. Once an agreement is reached, Youbet.com offers the track's races as part of the online menu it offers to account holders.

The trail blazing Youbet.com not only has the capabilities of bringing legal betting on horse races into peoples' homes, it also brings legal and legitimate closed-circuit broadcast signals of the races to the personal computer screens of account holders.

Even at a time when state and federal statutes relating to in-home wagering via telephonic communication and personal computers is still very unsettled and vague, the televising of races from tracks around the country is already up and running. It only makes sense that this is not for the pure viewing enjoyment of people. It is ultimately for wagering purposes.

The Racing Network (TRN), a Pennsylvania-based operation that was a joint effort between Canadian interests Greenwood Racing, Inc. and the Ontario Jockey Club, and Ladbroke Racing, was launched in 1999 and ceased operations in mid-2001. It was North America's first provider of multitrack, multichannel, 24-hour, direct-to-home racing coverage. California-based Television Games network (TVG) also debuted in 1999. Backed by TV Guide, Inc., the National Thoroughbred Racing Association, and AT&T Broadband and Internet Services, TVG launched operations with 12 hours of live racing coverage per day. Its impact has been increased with the partnership agreement it reached with Youbet.com. Panels of racing experts and handicappers who provide commentary and analysis host TVG.

According to Gutfreund, the opportunities made available to serious horseplayers through online wagering create interesting methods of attack. Is it advisable to spread yourself thin by looking at any number of tracks, or is it best to concentrate exclusively on one track and devote all of your energy, statistical input, and powers of observation to it?

"What works for one person does not necessarily work for someone else," Gutfreund maintains. "It is a matter of preference and comfort. If concentrating on one track works, then it is advisable to stick with it and not dilute your time by looking at other tracks. My personal preference is to make 'choice plays' at different tracks, particular horses that my method pinpoints. This process may uncover only a few horses during the course of a day's races but, if you bet wisely, it can prove to be a successful system."

Many handicappers opt for fields of specialization within the sport itself. For example, some experts prefer to concentrate on turf (grass) races, some on maiden (non-winners) races, some on claiming races (horses entered to be sold), some on allowance (high caliber) races, some on stakes and handicap (highest caliber) races.

Then there are categories within categories. For example, certain levels of claiming or allowance races, distance races or sprint races, horses returning to the races after a layoff, horses going up in class, horses going down in class, significant jockey changes, horses making their first starts for a new trainer after being claimed, 2-year-old races, favorites, long shots and many, many more.

For players who like to confine their particular field of expertise to a category, such as those listed above, the chance to study races and make plays at tracks around the country opens up broad new horizons for them. When confined to a single track at which to play, maybe one or two categorical opportunities would be presented each day and the race(s) could prove to be unplayable. When you're working with a number of tracks, you are able to scan the past performances for the races that interest you, then select the playable races according to your handicapping technique.

Say you are a handicapper who has chosen to specialize in turf races. On any given day, depending on the time of year and the weather, a track may have none, one or several grass races among the nine- or 10-race program. Online wagering opens up the opportunity to select from tracks around the country that will bring the number of races you choose to look at much higher. The same holds true for every subcategory of handicapping.

The wide variety of tracks and racing made available through online wagering is complemented by the vast storehouse of knowledge that is available on the Internet to serious handicappers. Databases and resource material that a few short years ago were hard to get, let alone even available to the general public, are now at every handicapper's fingertips. There are any number of sources available to obtain past performances of horses, breeding information, news and updates, handicapping advice and analysis (be very careful here), plus the luxury of being able to watch video replays of past races run at every track.

Selected information is free, some involves a fee. But if you are serious about betting the horses on the Internet, the more valuable information you obtain the better. So few individuals invest the time and effort to take advantage of optimum wagering opportunities in racing that such an investment is likely to return dividends multi-fold. It is similar to playing casino blackjack. By learning basic strategy and some form of card counting, you will become a better blackjack player than 99 percent of people who play the game.

Gutfreund acknowledges that not only is there more information available to interested parties today, there is much more *good* information. This is a very important factor. Because something is labeled "information" doesn't necessarily make it good or even factual. In the past, much of the information made available for sale to horseplayers amounted to the uneducated opinions and advice of touts simply out to make a quick buck. Just as in casino gambling, the buyer must be very wary of get-rich-quick scheme sellers.

Sure evidence of the availability of higher-quality information is the fact that the traditional tip sheets written by such characters as "Long-shot Larry," "Dr. Winner" and "The Tipster"; sheets which were so much a part of racetrack color and folklore, have begun to disappear. They have been replaced by legitimate statistical sources of information and analyses compiled by certified experts.

This doesn't mean that the hucksters have entirely disappeared. Many of them have taken their business online by selling their selections over the Internet. Don't fall for their lofty claims and guarantees. Before you pay for anybody else's selections, find out the handicapper's background. Search to find endorsements or comments made about the site in chat rooms devoted to horse racing enthusiasts.

Gutfreund cautions that it is important not to abuse the convenience and availability of betting on the horses online. He says that managing your account wisely is vital if you are looking to be a successful handicapper.

"If you don't exercise self-control you're going to wind up in financial trouble," Gutfreund says. "When there is a race every few minutes or so, you must choose your spots wisely. You must be careful not to get caught up with the ease of betting. Self-discipline is very important. Just because it's easier doesn't mean you play more than what is comfortable for you. Don't forget, just as with other forms of gambling, there is a good deal of luck involved over the short term. The long term is a different story. The astute, intelligent handicapper has a very good chance to come out ahead."

Wagering online is easy and very user-friendly with just basic computer skills. Navigation is quite simple. All that's required is to obtain a user ID and a password by logging onto the provider's website or calling the toll free telephone number. The software can be installed from a CD-ROM. Youbet.com even offers an express operating system that requires no CD. After that it's just a matter of connecting to your access provider (AOL, AT&T, Earthlink, Worldnet, etc.). From there you'll go to connect and you'll be off to the races once your wagering account is established.

Unlike casino gambling, there is no fear of putting your finances in danger when you establish an online horse betting account. Your money never leaves the country. Furthermore, it's legal under prevailing standards. The money that is taken out of your account is wagered through the track you are betting. What's more, you are paid full track odds, less a commission.

"This is just the beginning," Gutfreund maintains. "It is only going to get better and more convenient. Once state and federal issues are addressed, things will move along quickly. The quality of the video signal will be improved as will the quality of service and amenities made available to horse racing fans."

A Perspective on Online Wagering

There is a very important distinction to make at this time between online casino gambling and online horse race wagering. When you log onto an online casino, you go into a *virtual* casino environment and are subject to the whims and shortcomings of the sites that are out there. In many cases, it is much better to go to a real brick-and-mortar casino where you'll get a much fairer shake and enjoy the edges all serious and intelligent gamblers look for.

When you wager on horse races online through a reputable service such as Youbet.com, you are actually bringing the *real racetracks* right into your own home. All of the conveniences and advantages of being at the track are right there with you in the comfort of your living room. If anything, the quality of information that is available to you is better than being at the track. All you are sacrificing is the enjoyment of being live at the races and the commission you pay for the service.

With this truth established, it is important to remember that handicapping thoroughbred horse races is more of an art than a science. There are just too many variables to approach it as a science. As much information as you can absorb from statistical information and past performance lines, what happens if your horse breaks from the gate slowly, throws his rider, gets blocked by an opponent or stumbles on the turn?

It's a fact that handicapping races requires skill and a great deal of cerebral input because, unlike casino games, with the noteworthy exception of blackjack, what happens in the past in a thoroughbred racehorse's record can very definitely have an effect on that horse's future performance. Yet, even though statistics should be heavily relied upon, always remember that the figures should be used only as a guide and not as a Gospel. Learning to read between the lines, and using empirical reasoning in your handicapping process, will prove to be invaluable tools over the long run.

One very good reason that you cannot hope to derive scientific conclusions from a lot of the data involving a racehorse's past performance statistics is that much of that data is really approximation. Points of call, for example, or the position of horses at various points in the race and the lengths behind the leader, are made by a person (called a trackman) looking through binoculars giving dictation to a call taker. Fractional running times of horses are based on this data. Only the leader's time is technically accurate. All of the horses behind the leader at any point of call have fractional and finish times based on the number of lengths they were positioned behind the leader. In thoroughbred racing, a length is equal to a fifth of a second. Any error in approximating the distance between horses in lengths is magnified from the second horse to the last-place finisher.

Let's look at an example: Say that a horse wins a six furlongs race by 10 lengths and that his finish time was a minute and ten seconds (1:10). The runner-up's time will be recorded as a minute and twelve seconds (remember that one length is equal to a fifth of a second) or 1:12. But is that the actual time? In order for it to be actual it must be assumed the horse finished the race running at an even rate. But this is a highly improbable assumption. In the time it took the runner-up to reach the finish line after the winner's nose broke the electronic beam, he may very well have slowed down or per-

haps he speeded up, which alters the horse's individual running time.

The bottom line is to not base your handicapping decisions entirely on figure handicapping. Don't miss betting a
winner because his figure was a fraction of a point lower than
the horse you did wind up betting.

You'll quickly discover that a lot of what you are able
to decipher by reading between the lines will be derived from
your own powers of observation, and that's where online betting and having accessibility to videotaped runnings of past
races as well as the input of the eyes and ears of an expert live
at the track can return major dividends.

Leonardo da Vinci implored human beings to "learn
how to see." Many times we look but we really don't see. You
can see a car driving down the street, but what color was it?
What was the license plate number? What make was the car?
Was the driver a man or a woman? The same applies to
watching a horse race. It is important to learn how to watch a
horse race, and that starts by paying attention to horses other
than the one you bet on. It can be difficult to train your eye to
do this, since having a financial interest in a horse will natu-
rally rivet your attention on that animal.

But in watching your own horse so intently, you will
miss everything else that's going on in the race. What's more,
you tend to magnify and exaggerate things, good and bad,
that happen to your horse and you tend to place too much
emphasis on those occurrences the next time the horse runs.

When you are only able to attend the races once a week
or so, you miss out on many subtle aspects of horse races.
Many of these subtle happenings are not documented, which
means you had to be there to know. If you were there, and do
have this knowledge, it can give you a tremendous advantage
over your competition. And remember, your competition in
pari-mutuel horse racing is not the house but your fellow bettors . . . you are wagering against *them*.

When you are privy to information only a select group of people know, you are in possession of knowledge truly worth knowing. On the other hand, information that everybody knows really isn't worth knowing at all. Most of what everyone knows is written in black and white in a horse's past performance record. What only a few people know is hidden between the lines.

Handicapping 2-Year-Old Races: Horizons Unlimited

The history of sports is replete with rags-to-riches stories. There are numerous Horatio Alger tales about individuals who rose from obscure, humble beginnings to become legends on the field of athletic competition.

Such giants as Johnny Unitas, who was plucked out of sandlot semipro games to become one of the greatest NFL quarterbacks of all time; Mike Piazza, an afterthought, throwaway draft pick who has forged a reputation as one of the top catchers in major league baseball history; Kurt Warner, a one-time arena football player who crashed NFL headlines by leading the St. Louis Rams to victory in the 2000 Super Bowl.

Diamonds in the rough they are called. But such stories are by no means restricted to human athletic endeavor. The wonderful world of thoroughbred horse racing also has a representative array of inspirational stories.

John Henry, for instance, was just another horse, racing at obscure tracks in Louisiana, before his prowess became known. He went on to make a name for himself as one of the greatest ever, winning two Arlington Millions, two Horse of the Year titles, millions of dollars and the hearts of racing fans worldwide.

Or how about Nodouble, a handicap champion from the 60s. In his very first career race he was entered to be purchased for $7,500. He went on to win numerous big money events around the country, rising to the top of the handicap class before embarking on a career as one of the sport's most successful and prolific sires.

The history books are filled with stories of thorough-breds that sold for hundreds of thousands of dollars as year-lings, based on their conformation and royal bloodlines, who were never heard from again on the racetrack. On the other hand, there are stories about thoroughbreds that were ignored in the sales ring but who thundered to illustrious and profitable track careers.

Time and time again these words of wisdom ring true: You can't measure heart. The intangibles of spirit, desire, and the sheer will to succeed just cannot be revealed in cold sta-tistics. Such virtues are uncovered only when it comes time for the real test, the field of battle.

Thoroughbreds may begin racing when they are two years of age, even though many owners and trainers choose not to race their horses at such a tender age. Some experi-enced horsemen will argue that the animal's bones are not yet knit, the musculature is still developing and the proper disci-pline and demeanor aren't there yet.

Since all thoroughbreds celebrate a universal birthday on January 1 each year, 2-year-olds are not really two years old. A colt born in April, for example, will be considered a year old the following January and a 2-year-old the January after that. *Even at such a young age, it can be said that 2-year-old racing is the truest and most formful of all thoroughbred competition.* But how can this be, you ask, if it is true that "a horse's future can be judged by his past?" How is it possible to "handicap" a horse if there are no past performance charts from which to draw conclusions and formulate statistics?

Every racehorse at one time in his life had to race for the very first time. The only information available at this time is the following: parentage (bloodlines), morning workout times, auction price, and physical appearance. On the other hand, there are telltale signs when an established racehorse is approaching his best form: a solid last race, a series of progressively better efforts, a change in distance, class, rider or trainer, just to name a few.

But a first time starter, or a youngster that has made only one or two starts? Now that's a challenge! Or is it? It has been my experience that 2-year-old racing presents some of the very best opportunities in the sport to pick a winner. Here's why:

Just as in human athletic endeavor, the unbridled enthusiasm of the youngsters in the racing world is something to behold. The careers of both human athletes and equine athletes are so very comparable: Children start out playing for the sheer enjoyment of the game, then for school pride and eventually for professional fulfillment and monetary gain. So it is with 2-year-old thoroughbred race horses.

Thoroughbreds are born to run, a trait never better exemplified than when they are 2-year-olds. They run for the sheer joy of running. Their inherent competitive spirit almost takes a back seat to the giddy qualities they exhibit when they run free: heels kicking, head tossing, ears pricking, straining against the bit, nickering and enjoying life to the fullest.

It's an easy time for young thoroughbreds to be footloose and fancy free, just as it is with the human species. They have no worries or cares, no aches or pains. They haven't become jaded to the ways of the world, nor have they developed bad habits or lost the spark of discovery.

Of the 20,000 or so thoroughbreds that are foaled every year, roughly half of them will ever make it to the races. The remainder will spend their lives as pleasure horses, show horses or hunters and jumpers. It's kind of like minor league baseball players and college football players. Only a small percentage of them will ever make it to the big leagues of professional sports.

Just as it is a major accomplishment for a thoroughbred to become an accomplished race horse, of the youngsters that do make it to the starting gate only a small percentage of them will ever become career runners. Some will be injured and retired, destined for the show ring or a pleasure stable. Still others will never win a race as flaws in their spirit of competition or their physical makeup are uncovered.

On the other side of the 2-year-old fence are the bettors, handicappers and racing fans who watch them run. Experienced race-watchers will tell you that 2-year-old races present prime opportunities at the betting windows. And there is no better time than now to take advantage of this fact on the Internet.

For openers, all 2-year-olds start out on an even field of competition. In a race matching a dozen youngsters making their first career starts will be horses who'll go on to distinguished careers as stake horses; others who'll become mid-class allowance horses, and still others who will occupy the role of the foot soldiers of the racing world, the claiming horses. Some will specialize as sprinters, others will prefer a distance of ground. You just never know at this juncture. Who will become the standouts and who will be the journeymen? With no past performances to bank on, nobody really knows for sure. It's a phenomenon that bettors will never encounter again. It's a brief window of opportunity that you must be quick to discover. As horses progress in their careers, their abilities become clearly established. Horses of relative equal skills are matched against one another to make for more competitive racing.

The opportunity that exists to pinpoint a horse far superior in ability to his competition is one of the delightful aspects of handicapping 2-year-old races. It's the only class of thoroughbred competition in which this is even possible to do, and one which fans of the sport and those learning the convenience of online betting should exercise.

In 2-year-old racing, it's not uncommon to see a youngster blow away his opponents. His inherent championship quality was hidden, incapable of being exposed by statistics and data. It was revealed only when he was placed in the heat of competition. Even the horse's connections, his owner, trainer, even jockey, can be fooled. Fast workers in the early dawn hours that race sluggishly in the afternoon are known as morning glories. Conversely, some horses that have been totally uninterested during training hours storm the track like tigers when they break from the gate under racing conditions.

If you limit your online betting activity to 2-year-old racing, primarily in the late spring, summer and early fall, making it a habit to concentrate on all the maiden, maiden special-weight and maiden-claiming races at tracks nation-wide, you will have discovered a potential gold mine that previously was unavailable to adventurous handicappers. Here are some key past performance factors that should trigger a betting alarm in your head each and every time you see them:

1. Be on the lookout for youngsters who drop out of the maiden special weight ranks into a maiden claimer regardless of the form they have exhibited. Maiden special weight races are generally far superior to their claiming cousins. Two-year-olds have a tendency to improve dramatically with this particular drop and the price can be right, especially when the lone race or two in the higher elevations was a dud.

2. Watch for a 2-year-old who was bet down to low odds in his first career start and didn't win. There was a reason for that heavy betting action to show. If the general public didn't have access to the info, that meant the horse's insiders did. If the connections thought that much of the horse the first time out of the box, it makes perfect sense to give the animal another chance. Again, depending on the quality of the horse's losing debut, the price can be very inviting.

3. Scout juveniles who come out of races which were captured by exceptionally impressive winners. Remember the race, then tab all of the 2-year-olds that finished behind the winner, especially those which were prominent during the early running. You'll be surprised how many winners such a ploy will produce.

4. Finally, always remember that youngsters can improve dramatically from one start to another. Speed is the foundation of all classic race horses. If a first time starter exhibits high octane speed for half a mile, then abruptly stops and winds up getting soundly beaten, by all means watch that horse the next time out. Unlike older, established horses, which stop because of physical infirmities or attitude problems, 2-year-olds stop because they simply needed the race. Next time out, they benefit greatly from the experience and not only run farther, they often go all the way to victory at handsome mutuels.

Expanded Handicapping Advice

Online horse racing and betting, as well as selected Internet services and capabilities, make it possible to enjoy the luxury of being there even when you're not. The power a bettor has of watching races and making observations known as trip notes is a glorious one. It enables those willing to capitalize on situations that are known only to a select few to make the kind of scores that separate horse race investors from horse players. Let's take a moment to expand on some of those key situations.

If you choose to concentrate on target races at a number of tracks instead of all the races at one track, here are some ideas to contemplate:

1. Trainer and Jockey Patterns: While it can prove frustrating to attempt to figure out what horses are trying to tell us, there is definitely some validity to putting stock in the human element of the sport, jockeys and trainers. Trainers follow patterns of predictable behavior and it is often possible to use some handicapping deductive reasoning to figure out what a trainer is trying to do. Some trainers can tip their hands and reveal their intentions in the manner in which they bring a horse up to winning potential. The pattern is repeated over and over again. Locking into this method can yield nice long-term profits. How about jockeys? Riding styles are often suited to particular running styles. Key in on the right matches by following jockey changes and you'll be on to something good.

2. Golden Runners-Up: Here is one where you'll be required to do a little reading between the lines. Check the top three finishers on each line of a horse's past performance. Look for races in which the winner won by a slim margin over the second horse who in turn was lengths in front of the third horse. This always is a sign of a very solid effort by the runner-up, even though the winner got the money and all the glory. Why? If the second horse in defeat was that much better than the third horse, his race was almost as good as the winner's. Such efforts tend to get overlooked. Make it a point to tab those good-as-gold runners-up.

3. Key Races: Just as select 2-year-old races can produce a lot of winners next time out from the field of also-rans, so can some races for older horses. They can become what I call key races. It is uncanny sometimes how many winners will come out of certain races. Perhaps it was a particularly contentious event, maybe there was a mitigating circumstance such as a spill. Whatever the reason, if you see an inordinate number of horses come back out of the same race to run big the next time out, circle that race and tab all of the horses who make their next starts after it.

4. Horses for Courses: It's a tired old phrase that has worn out its welcome in many respects in today's modern racing picture, but it still can come into play. Some horses run better at certain tracks. In years past, prior to expanded information in a horse's past performance chart, astute handicappers could keep their own mental notes of this phenomenon and collect generous returns when the horse would return to his favorite track. Now individual performance over race tracks is a matter of public information. But even so, if a horse hasn't been running particularly well of late and suddenly turns up at a track over which he has enjoyed previous success, the chances are good he'll come up with a vastly improved effort at his old stomping grounds.

5. Class: As I have already established, knowledge that everybody knows isn't worth knowing. In conjunction with this, we come to the subject of class. The betting public at large generally jumps on horses going down in class and stays away from horses going up in class. A dropper will always get an inordinate amount of play, often taking away any value the horse may have as a betting prospect. On the other hand, a class riser will always get less play than he would have at the level he raced last time which often creates better betting value.

To take advantage of this particular target race, it is wise to string along with in-form horses stepping up in class and off-form horses dropping in class. A horse that has solid recent races and suddenly drops in class will attract too much play. Very often, such form makes for a very weak favorite and one you can bet against. The horse with the poor recent races may be the one to watch on the drop, even though he won't lure excessive betting action. People tend to overlook animals with poor recent form, but that's the very time a horse should be dropped in class. If the horse isn't making money at his present level of competition, doesn't it make sense to try a different level to get those purse checks rolling in? Horses who step up after winning are often lightly regarded by the betting public, yet this is often the time to jump on the bandwagon and make hay (and cash tickets!) while the sun shines. It's a sign the horse is sharp, in form, and capable of handling the class hike to a higher level of earning power. One good barometer to check is the seasonal earnings of the horse in question. If a horse has made a lot of money, yet drops into a race far below what his established earning power is, it's a good sign the horse may be slipping. If a horse doesn't exhibit good earning power and is dropping in class, it's a good sign that it could be time to bet. The horse's connections are just searching for that strike force level to get the animal to pay some bills.

6. Track Bias: This one can take a lot of work but it can also be well worth your time and effort. By observing signals from the different tracks on a day-to-day basis and making note of track conditions, which part of the track was best and whether the surface was favoring speed or stretch runners, you can create a database that will make you an outstanding investor in horse racing futures. If you make note of the speed horses who tired on a day the track favored stretch runners, you can find inviting prices in their next races. Conversely, scouting stretch runners who failed to make up their usual ground on tracks favoring speed can also be good bets the next time out. You can take this particular online target race category a step further. If a horse won a race on a speed-favoring track, then turns up the favorite the next time on a neutral track or a strip favoring closers, the horse could be a hollow chalk and could be well worth betting against. The same holds true for false favorites in the stretch runner category. Similarly, if a horse lost a race while bogged down in a deeper portion of the track, he can be worth betting back if you're just willing to throw the race out. If a horse narrowly won while enjoying all the benefits of the best part of the track and gets bet down heavily off that win next time out, he could be worth betting against because his strength may be an apparition. In another vein, in a bygone era it used to be worth making note of mudders and horses who favor the grass, but now those stats are kept for you in the form of expanded past performance information. If everybody knows it, you will gain no edge.

7. Conditions: It never hurts to follow the classification of horses, even though it has lost its impact with the expanded information available to players. Always watch for 3-year-olds coming out of a race against older opponents to take on their own age group, especially early in the year. Similarly, tab up-and-comers who may have been out of their element in a non-winners of three races lifetime dropping to the next level, a non-winners of two races.

8. Empirical Angles: Sometimes if you concentrate on generalities rather than specifics, you can uncover easy-to-find angles at race tracks around the country to take advantage of your online wagering capabilities. Solid angles such as the ones I list have produced positive results through the years even though it is tough to explain just how they work. For example, tab distance runners who come off sprint races and tab sprinters who come off distance races. Quite often trainers will use such races to shake their horses out of the doldrums. A quick sprint will sharpen up a closer, while a distance race can leg up a sprinter. A very lucrative angle can be dirt horses that come out of turf (grass) races. For some empirical reason, a horse gets sharpened up significantly when returning to the dirt after a turf tightener. Finally, watch for horses dropping out of what are classified as starter allowance races. Starter allowances are open to horses of varying class. Often it can attract a runner who is far superior to his opponents and thereby create hidden value in horses the next time they compete at a more definable level, such as a claiming race with a set value.

9. Value: The beauty of pari-mutuel wagering is that you bet against one another and not the house, which means there is no standard house edge working against you such as in casino games like roulette, craps and blackjack to a lesser degree. Horse racing invites wise players to shop for value in any given race. Many times it is possible to wager on a horse not because you think he is the best horse in the race but because he exhibits the best value. This is taking supreme advantage of the pari-mutuel system. Let me explain. If you think a horse should be 5 to 1 odds but you look up and see he is 2 to 1 on the board, there is no value here and he is not worth betting. If on the other hand you figure a horse should be 2 to 1 in odds and you look up and see that he is 5 to 1, this presents excellent value and can be a dandy wagering proposition. If you shop for value in races at tracks around the country, you are bucking the odds as well as the percentage takeout.

Sportsbooks

Betting on college and professional sports over the Internet opens up new areas of discussion not covered in the casino gambling and horse racing sections of this book. Even though betting on the outcome of sporting events is legal in this country only in the state of Nevada, this activity is practiced illegally in one form or another by a large segment of the population. What's more, betting on sports is not only a condoned activity, it is actually encouraged by the information provided in daily newspapers and various other publications and media outlets.

Remember that pari-mutuel betting on horse races is legal in many states. Newspapers in markets that have live horse racing will usually devote space in the sports pages to handicapping analysis and expert selections. But just as much space, or even more, is filled with betting lines and point spreads, over-under lines and expert picks on the college and professional sports that happen to be in season at the time. What does this type of information serve other than to provide bettors with information? Talk about hypocrisy!

Whereas betting on sports is often very much out in the open in the form of office pools, fantasy leagues and the like, any form of illegal casino gambling activity is strictly underground. Yet casino gambling of one form or another, as well as lotteries, are now legal in many states. God help any business owner who gets caught with a blackjack or dice table in the back room, but meanwhile, the office pool during the

NCAA's March Madness has hundreds of dollars at stake and nobody bats an eye. It is overlooked as a harmless activity, which in fact it probably is. But in essence is it really any different than betting over the phone with a bookie? I think not.

What about the information that's available in newspapers across the country during the college and professional football season? Page after page is filled with game-by-game analysis, injury reports, charts, straight up picks and picks with the spread. There are even special sections devoted to information that only a person interested in gambling on the games would care about, not stories and sidebars that fans look for.

Gambling on sports is a given in American society. At times, talk has even surfaced about making it legal, but such talk quickly fades away. With this perspective in mind, the Internet is filled with sites devoted to betting on sports. They are very similar to online casino gambling sites, and in some instances they even are part of the same site. As with casino gambling sites, they are registered out of foreign countries to skirt the legality issues that exist within the boundaries of the United States.

When you go to an online sports book, your account is set up in much the same way as a casino gambling account. The big difference between casino gambling online and sports betting online is that when you log onto a casino site you remain there to interactively play games, while when you log onto a sports book you plug in your betting information on an online form.

A wide variety of sports betting is offered online, including baseball, football, basketball, hockey, soccer, tennis, boxing, motor sports and golf. The offerings even span the globe with such sports as rugby and cricket. Even horse racing is available. If you are inclined to wager on sports, there certainly is no lack of information about the games available at your fingertips and for a reasonable cost.

The variety of bets and wagering propositions that are offered on these sites is a veritable cornucopia, including straight bets, parlay wagering, parlay cards, teasers, sweetheart teasers, futures and if bets, among others. As with online casino gambling there are sign up perks and bonuses, low minimum deposits and low minimum bets. It's just a matter of logging on to a search engine and checking out the sites that appeal to you. There is also the inherent danger of dishonest sites, so be very careful how and with whom you spend your gambling dollars.

Online sports betting is very different from casino betting because you have the ability to handicap the games, using the information that is readily available to you. You also have the time to study the match-ups and make your wagering decisions at a leisurely pace. Similar cautions are also in force. If you spread yourself too thin, and start making plays all over the place on a multitude of games, you are asking for trouble. The convenience that online sports betting makes possible should not plant seeds of self (not to mention bankroll) destruction in your gambling behavior.

The manner in which you handicap sports betting varies depending on the sport. For sports like baseball, basketball and hockey, all of which have long seasons and big schedules, the intensity of the games can wax and wane. In baseball the pitching match-ups are of prime concern. In basketball home court advantage must be factored in.

Football, both college and pro, is an entirely different situation. Teams play once a week, not every day as in baseball. Each and every game that's played can impact a team's season. A single loss for a college team can squash its chances for a shot at the national title. The games are played with much more intensity. Rivalries very often neutralize spreads. Up-to-the minute injury reports can prove to be vital information for bettors.

College basketball also differs from professional basketball, again mainly on the intensity and school rivalry areas. Because sports betting deals with people and personalities, the emotional factor weighs heavy on the decision-making process when it comes to making a bet.

By becoming a student of one sport, rather than a "jock of all trades," you are more likely to make intelligent online betting decisions rather than making wagers just for the action. Pursuing it seriously takes a great deal of time and effort, just as horse race handicapping does, but there is enough solid information available to make it worthwhile for the committed player.

Certainly betting sports online is preferable to doing business with your neighborhood bookie. Just exercise the proper precautions and self discipline.

I mentioned that wagering on horse races is available online in sportsbooks, but my advice is to steer clear of it. As I established earlier, a service such as Youbet.com is a legal online service operated within the boundaries of the United States. Wagers are deducted from the individual's account and transmitted directly into the wagering pools at the tracks via the Ladbroke hub in Pennsylvania. You are also assured of getting track odds. Wagering on horse races with an offshore betting service creates risks that are not necessary for you to take.

Sports bettors will find Bettor's World (*www.bettorsworld.com*) a very useful resource for sports betting information, links to sites, news and online sports book reviews. Always remember that when a site accepts advertising as this one does, you must be discriminating when it comes to using the information. The real value in this type of site is that it's an easy way to link to a variety of online sportsbooks when you are searching for one. There is also online casino information available at Bettors World, but the main reason for visiting will be if you are interested in wagering on sports.

Steering Clear of Online Scams and Con Artists

In addition to all of the legitimate sites related to gambling on the Internet, there is also a whole lot of garbage out there. There are always going to be sharpies attempting to extract money from gullible people who think that by purchasing inside information and advice they'll get the winning edge. The same con men who utilize mass-mailings to disseminate get-rich-quick schemes also have jumped on the Internet and purchased websites to advertise their wares and services.

This is not meant to disparage some of the good information that is available from genuine experts and authorities. In order to distinguish the phonies from the real thing, simply scan through the site and check out the purveyor's credentials. Bragging rights don't count here, because it's easy to make false boasts and fiddle with statistics. Check out the cost of the service and how long it has been operational. Try to get feedback from other people who may have used it.

My point is that there is so much good information available for free, or for a nominal cost relating to all casino, sports and horse-race wagering online, that you should put stock in your own intellect and accumulate and digest the information yourself. Horse racing, in particular, has a multitude of online resources to obtain program pages from tracks around the country and past performances of every horse in training. Prior to the Internet, this prime information was never so readily available.

There are touts associated with every form of gambling. They even exist in financial circles, only they operate under the guise of advisors and financial analysts. Football season is loaded with experts seeking to put you on winning parlays and can't miss "games of the week." Horse racing has its fair share of handicappers eager to pick "sure things" for you, as well. You'll know the phony sites when you find them. The boasts and guarantees of success are a sure give-away.

When it comes to the multitude of advertisements for online casinos that you'll encounter while surfing the various sites, keep in mind that the sites have their own little deals going. Let me explain. When a player signs on to an online casino by clicking on an affiliate link, the referring webmaster is usually in line to receive a finders fee that is based on a percentage of any losses incurred by the player. That's why you see so many advertisements and so many online casino links on the sites you'll run across.

All advertising is self serving, but in the regulated business world there has to be truth in advertising, and the purveyors of the goods and services must be held account-able for the claims that they make. In the Internet gaming industry, what's for sale to the public is the opportunity to gamble online. Under its present structure, online players are not given any guarantees. Therefore, always take online casi-no advertising claims with a grain of salt and a wary eye, knowing that online casino entrepreneurs are looking to make money off your experience every step of the way.

Lotteries, Bingo, Etc.

In my estimation, lotteries amount to nothing more than state-sanctioned numbers rackets. The politicians in their never ending quest to bring new revenue into state coffers simply took the underground numbers game away from the neighborhoods, wrapped it up in a pretty bow, and legitimized it. A lottery is still the numbers racket, only worse.

I suppose you have guessed by now that lottery mania has also come to the Internet. There are sites to not only play the game, but also ones where lottery fans can get information and results from lotteries worldwide.

One such site, Lottery America (*www.lotteryamerica.com*), will give you winning numbers worldwide dating back to 1989. There are state, as well as foreign country links. You are able to discover what numbers won on what days, or you can even find out if a set of numbers you key in has ever been drawn. There are links to services and ads for software, too.

It seems a fruitless enterprise to me to use the Internet for something as frivolous as lotteries. The luck factor makes all databases meaningless, so why bother?

As for Bingo players, you would have to be a real fan of the game to pursue it online, especially with the availability of the live game in so many states. Nevertheless, there are a number of cyber Bingo halls in which people play against one another online for prizes and progressive jackpots.

Again, we're talking about a no brainer here except for whatever entertainment value people derive from it.

WorldWinner.com (*www.worldwinner.com*) has come up with an interesting online approach for people who like to play games of skill, such as Solitaire, Free Cell, Minesweeper, jigsaw puzzles, crossword puzzles, chess, checkers and more, and like to bet money on the outcome. Since this approach utilizes skill, the company markets itself as the first legal alternative to online gambling for U.S. Internet users. Participants sign up to play by depositing money in their account with a credit card. Players may register for daily tournaments as well as progressives, which are based on the number of entrants. WorldWinner makes its money with a rake of the entry fees.

We're not talking high stakes here, either. Some of the entry fees are as little as 60 cents with prizes ranging from $2.00 and up. If you're interested, you can register with a deposit of as little as $5.00 and have some online fun. Navigating the site is a little cumbersome, but if you're a fan of the games they offer, and would like to play with a little added incentive (money!) and excitement, it may be worth a visit.

Section 2

Tips on Choosing an Internet Casino

With the vast number of Internet casinos from which to choose, what's a player to do? There is precious little objective information available. Most of what the majority of people know about particular online casinos is what they are told in advertising. But what value can we place on facts that are, to be quite honest, the best information that money can buy?

The situation is ultimately complicated by the fact that the online casino gambling industry is unregulated and conducted under the auspices of bodies that do not necessarily place the best interests of the public at the top of the list. Internet gambling is second only to adult-oriented sites in the profits that it generates. There is a tremendous amount of money to be made by the people who launch Internet gambling sites. Still, being motivated by profit is not necessarily bad, and there is a lot of money being made by an elite group of Internet casino owners and operators.

With the number of online gambling casinos growing every day, there is tremendous competition for players. Just about all online casinos, according to their own promotional teasers, offer the biggest bonuses, the best odds and the broadest variety of games. But do they? They want your business and they'll do anything to grab your attention. Since they are not really held accountable for the claims they make, the ultimate judge and jury of whether they survive is the public they serve.

As I have mentioned, the only regulation in the Internet casino gambling industry has surfaced from within. The industry has done an admirable job policing itself, but when it comes to choosing an online casino the most solid advice is "Let the Player Beware."

The very medium over which people engage in online gambling can ultimately be their best friend. By searching the world wide web for online gambling related sites, chat rooms, independent sources and all and any other objective information that is available, you'll be doing everything you can do to assure yourself safe adventures into the myriad of cyber-space casinos.

With that said, I would like to offer some advice about how to narrow your search for an online casino. Investing the time, effort, and money it requires to investigate each online casino would prove to be a dauntless yet disappointing enterprise. The persistent law of diminishing returns will create an avalanche of questionable information that will bury any good you derive from your quest.

Which brings us to this undeniable and all-important truth: *Even though there are hundreds upon hundreds of individual online casinos, there are but a select number of software providers. Even though the sites have different names and different looks, the vast majority of them are governed by the parameters and game characteristics that are given to them by the main software providers.*

Therefore, our analysis of the sites will not center on the individual online casinos, but rather on the software providers which make them work, govern the rules of play and create different playing situations and climates. By zeroing in on distinguishing characteristics among the software providers, we'll then be able to focus on the casinos as groups rather than as individual sites.

It is also important to be aware of the fact that in isolated cases some software providers permit their license holders to modify the rules on the games they offer, such as the number of decks used at blackjack, so always be on the alert. Know the rules of every game you play before you invest your hard-earned money.

For the purposes of our discussion, I'll target the following software providers, which constitute our "Select Seven" providers in the online gambling industry: Gambling Software.com, Starnet, Microgaming, Unified Gaming, Real Time Gaming, Boss Media and Cryptologic.

They are not the only software providers that are out there, but they are among the major ones with the most sites in their online casino arsenal.

My findings and opinions are by no means an endorsement of the software providers. They represent facts and information as I know them. Highlighting them is merely a tool to make our search for an online casino much easier. If you like certain features about a provider, you can seek the online casinos they service. If you dislike certain features about a provider, you can avoid online casinos they service. It's that simple.

A majority of the software providers are privately held companies. The technology, variety of games and video and audio enhancements are in a constant state of change. By logging on to the company websites of the various software providers, you'll be able to pick up a lot of information about the companies as well as have the opportunity to see the games they provide.

In addition to learning about the games and software that they offer, you'll be able to find out what country the company is based in and contact information. I encourage you to call the providers with any questions you may have about the games they offer. The provider answering one question speaks for many online casino sites. Some of them also provide a list of the online casinos to which they provide software.

At this point I'd like to also mention another great resource website: *www.gamblinglicenses.com*. This site provides a myriad of information about Internet casino operations as well as a complete listing of software providers and links to their websites.

Now let's get into some specific providers and highlights of their software:

Gambling Software.com
(www.gamblingsoftware.com)

A Java-based (no download) provider which offers good visuals and an excellent, user-friendly play format. The standard blackjack game uses four decks, but they are shuffled when approximately 80 percent of the cards are left. The dealer stands on soft 17 (a player friendly rule), but this perk is countered by the fact you cannot double down on any two cards. You may double down after splitting, but only once.

Be on guard when playing blackjack that if the dealer has a 10 showing and flips over an Ace for a blackjack, the player loses not only the entire bet but also any double down or split wagers. Surrender is not permitted.

There are seven different slot games, a multi-player format in Texas Hold'em, and video poker in addition to a variety of table poker games. Craps, roulette, Spanish 21 and Caribbean Stud Poker are also available as are Pull Tabs, which under no circumstances receive my playing endorsement. The video poker is a good Jacks or Better game with a $5.00 minimum and a 9-6 pay table (9-1 for a Full House, 6-1 for a Flush).

Some **Gambling Software.com** online casinos to look at include:

Casino Brio (*www.casinobrio.com*)

Place My Bet (*www.placemybet.net*)

Roman Palace Casino (*www.romanpalace.com*)

Treasures Casino (*www.treasurescasino.com*)

Living Casino (*www.livingcasino.com*)

Excelsior Casino (*www.excelsiorcasino.com*)

Sierra Gold Casino (*www.sierragoldcasino.com*)

Monte Casino (*www.montecasino.com*)

Pyramid Palace (*www.pyramidpalace.com*)

Vegas Grand (*www.vegasgrand.com*)

Players Fortune (*www.playersfortune.com*)

Pair of Dice (*www.pairofdice.com*)

Starnet
(www.starnetsystems.net)

Starnet-powered casinos are generally safe and reliable with user-friendly software. In addition to the usual complement of games, it offers Bingo (not recommended because of the outrageous hold percentages), Battle Royale, Pachinko, Sic Bo (which has a ridiculous house advantage), Red Dog, Pai Gow (a variation of Pai Gow Poker), Caribbean Poker (a.k.a. Caribbean Stud Poker) and Free Ride (a.k.a Let It Ride).

The blackjack game uses six decks. The dealer stands on soft 17 and the player may double down on any first two cards (a plus), however there is no doubling down after a split and no resplitting. A player loses his entire wager if the dealer has an Ace in the hole with a 10 showing.

There are four variations of video poker. The Jacks or Better game offers a less-than-generous 6/5 pay table. The other games are Deuces Wild, Joker Poker and King of the Deck.

Starnet's version of Casino War is attractive to players because in the event of a tie after going to war the payoff is 3 to 1.

Some **Starnet**-powered casinos to look at include:

Win4Real.com (*www.win4real.com*)

Players Casino (*www.playersonly.com*)

Club Rio Casino (*www.clubriocasino.com*)

Wincity casino (*www.wincitycasino.com*)

Superbet Casino (*www.surperbet.com*)

Microgaming
(www.microgaming.com)

Microgaming, established in 1994, is the oldest and one of the most reliable software providers out there. It was honored as the year's "Best Software Provider" by *Casino Player Magazine* based on the results of an online survey.

It is constantly introducing new technology. Its latest innovation is something they call minimum download software or MUP (Microgaming Upgrade Protocol) which allows players to initially download a small file containing a minimum number of games. While the customer is playing, the remaining games are downloaded automatically in the background.

Microgaming also has launched a website (*www.jackpotmadness.com*) which updates players about its jackpot network and provides links to affiliated casinos.

The blackjack game uses a single deck but that's where the good news ends. The dealer stands on soft 17, you can double down only on two-card totals of 9, 10 and 11, there's no doubling after splitting, no resplitting and no surrender. What's more, the player loses his full bet, including all double-down and split money, on any dealer blackjack.

Microgaming's craps game may not be an award winner, but it makes up for that shortcoming with single-zero roulette and a fine selection of video poker, including an inviting 9/6 Jacks or Better game.

Some **Microgaming** sites to check out include:

Floridita Club Casino (*www.floriditaclubcasino.com*)

UK Casino (*www.ukcasino.com*)

7 Sultans Casino (*www.7sultans.com*)

Jackpot City (*www.jackpotcity.com*)

Blackjack Ballroom (*www.blackjackballroom.com*)

Unified Gaming
(*www.unifiedgaming.com*)

This very popular provider of Java software offers one of the very best games of blackjack available in either single deck or 6-deck variety. How about these perks: The dealer stands on soft 17, the player may double on any two cards and double down after splitting. Players are permitted to split up to three times, with the exception of aces, and late surrender is available.

Unified's craps game is nothing special and the roulette is the tired double-zero wheel, but it has an outstanding Pai Gow Poker game and a wide variety of video poker games that vary from site to site. The Jacks or Better game sports a mediocre 8/5 pay table but the Deuces Wild variation is very good.

Selected **Unified Gaming** online casinos include:

5 Dimes Casino (*www.5dimes.com*)

Gamblers Palace (*www.gamblerspalace.com*)

Old Las Vegas Casino (*www.oldlasvegascasino.com*)

Vegas From Home (*www.vegasfromhome.com*)

Players Bet Casino (*www.playersbet.com*)

Real Time Gaming
(*www.realtimegaming.com*)

Organized in 1998, Real Time Gaming has come on strong in the online casino gaming industry. The software must be downloaded, but it is very user-friendly and quite attractive. Many Real Time Gaming clients use a two-deck blackjack game but that number can vary from site to site. The dealer hits soft 17 (a disadvantage to the player) but you are allowed to double down on any two cards, double after splitting and split up to three hands, all player perks.

Roulette players have the option of playing the American version (double zero) or the European version (single zero). Given a choice there is no argument; the single zero is the better one. Real Time Gaming also offers an outstanding and advantageous selection of video poker games, including 9/6 Jacks or Better.

Selected **Real Time Gaming** sites:

Casino Merlin (*www.casinomerlin.com*)

Club Regal Casino (*www.clubregalcasino.com*)

Las Vegas USA Casino (*www.lasvegasusacasino.com*)

The Casino Online (*www.thecasinoonline.com*)

PowerBet (*www.powerbet.com*)

Boss Media
(*www.bossmedia.com*)

A quality software provider with some outstanding games, including the best craps on the Internet. Players take up to three-times odds at craps and the graphics and ease of play are both outstanding.

Boss Media offers both single- and multi-player options. The 6-deck multi-player blackjack game has its pros and cons. On the plus side, the dealer stands on soft 17, players may double on any first two cards, they may double after splitting and players lose only their original wager in the event of a dealer blackjack. A minus is the fact there is no resplitting permitted. There is also a single-deck game available.

You won't want to go to a Boss Media–powered casino to play video poker, however. The only game available is Jacks or Better and it offers a stingy 7/5 pay table.

Select **Boss Media** sites:

Atlantic Casino (*www.atlanticcasino.com*)

California Casino (*www.californiacasino.com*)

Jackpot Palace (*www.jackpotpalace.com*)

Mini Vegas Casino (*www.minivegascasino.com*)

USA Casino (*www.usacasino.com*)

Cryptologic
(www.cryptologic.com)

An industry leader in multi-player games, Cryptologic offers very pleasing graphics and play action. The blackjack game is o.k. Eight decks are used, the dealer stands on soft 17, players may double on any first two cards and doubling after splitting is permitted. There is no surrender and pairs may be split only one time.

Cryptologic slot games are intriguing because some of its license holders reveal game payback percentage. However, one check of the figures reinforces my opinion that Internet casinos are definitely not the place for serious slot players.

The selection of video poker games isn't bad. The Jacks-or-Better variety offers the sought after 9/6 paytable.

Roulette players will find Cryptologic's game inviting because it offers half the player's money back on even money bets if the ball lands on zero or double zero.

Select **Cryptologic** sites include:

Casino Monte Carlo (*www.casinomontecarlo.com*)

William Hill Casino (*www.williamhillcasino.com*)

VIP Casino (*www.vipcasino.com*)

Omni Casino (*www.omnicasino.com*)

Las Vegas At Home Casino (*www.lasvegasathomecasino.com*)

In addition to the major software providers that I've highlighted here, there are a number of additional ones. Most of them are also very good and reliable. The online casino gambling industry is growing by leaps and bounds every day. The climate is ripe for new entries into the market, some of which will fail, some of which will just survive, and some of which will flourish.

Here are the names of more gambling software and system providers to look for when you are searching for an online casino: AC & G Software (Blackjack Champ), Access Gaming Systems, Action Sportsbook System, Autotote, Bet and Chat, BingoGold, Casino Age, Casino Builders, Casino Consult, Chartwell Technology, Cyberdealer Network, Inc., Diamond Games, dot com Entertainment Group, eSportzBook, Evergreen New Media, Fairplay Online BV, First Bingo, First Multimedia Group, GameHouse, Gaming and Entertainment Technology, Gaming Logix, Global Entertainment, Inc., Global Games, Global Interactive, G-Master, Goldplay Gaming Systems, Grand Virtual, iCrystal, iGamingSolutions, iGlobalMedia, IGS (Interactive Gaming Systems), iNet Software, Innoco, Intel game, Interactive Solutions Corporation, Internet Global Network, Inc., Intertainet Overseas Licensing, Intetronic Ltd., Intralot, IQ-Ludorum Plc and Kismet Studios.

Still other major suppliers are Las Vegas from Home.com Entertainment, Inc., LiveBet Online, Multi-Effective, Net Entertainment, Netorg AG – CasinoSoft4You, NewGold – PlayLink Inc., Next Generation Gaming,

NWDP.com, Odds On, OnGame, Online Gaming Systems, OwnCasino.com, Piramind, PlayStar, Poker.com, Radiate Software, Random Logic, Real Gambling Software, SportXction, Total Entertainment, Inc., Virtgame Corp., World Gaming Systems, Inc., WorldNet Gaming, Xirtrix Gaming Technologies, Inc. and Zootec.

There are also lots of smaller providers in cyberspace which, quite frankly, must earn your respect and trust. You're playing it as safe as you possibly can by sticking with the older, well-established companies which have a strong arsenal of proven cyber casino sites. You're taking enough of a chance by gambling in the first place. Why take more chances than you have to? Stick with proven, time-tested, and consumer endorsed properties.

Getting Personal with Selected Sites

Sands of the Caribbean
(www.thesands.com)

I love this casino and would recommend it to anybody. For openers, it meets my criteria for longevity (in business since August of 1997) and customer satisfaction. This is a huge casino with software provided by Cryptologic. The graphics are great and the site is easy to navigate. It is without a doubt one of the most popular and trusted online casinos.

I really liked the month-by-month payout table with audited reports of payback percentages for all the games it offers. There's 24-hour, seven-days-a-week customer support as well as a guarantee of account security. You can play penny, nickel and dime slots here. The selection of games is also very good.

The blackjack is nothing to brag about with eight decks that are shuffled after every hand. The paytables for the video poker games are a bit on the soft side, but for everything you can knock about the games you can certainly bank on Sands of the Caribbean for running an honest and time-tested site.

Intercasino
(www.intercasino.com)

This site has also been around for a long time, which, in this business, is one of the best endorsements you can get. For slot players there is a big variety of games, although I do not recommend playing slots online. There is a nice selection of video poker, too, but as is the case with many online casinos, the paytables leave much to be desired. The craps game is a very entertaining double odds game, but don't look for any bargains on bet payouts here. The game's fun factor is one thing. Taking it seriously as a gambler is quite another.

Club Monte Carlo
(www.clubmontecarlo.com)

If you don't visit this site for any other reason, you should check out the blackjack. It's a single-deck game in which the dealer stands on all 17s and you are permitted to double on any first two cards (but not after splitting). That's a good game of blackjack. The single-zero roulette is worth the trip, too.

William Hill Casino
(www.williamhillcasino.com)

It hasn't been in the Internet gambling business as long as Sands of the Caribbean, but with a name like William Hill Company (of British bookmaker fame) to back it up, it's easy to understand why this site has become one of the most trusted and popular.

The blackjack uses eight decks of cards which are shuffled after every hand and the video poker takes liberties with the pay tables, but there is an outstanding selection of good, honest games that you should have no qualms about playing.

Global-Player Casino
(www.global-player.com)

This site uses its own software, which gives it a unique quality. I must say that the graphics are some of the best I've seen and the playing experience is very entertaining.

I really appreciated the selection of blackjack games that it offers, including Vegas Strip (4 decks), Downtown Vegas (3 decks), Reno (3 decks), Atlantic City (6 decks), Baden-Baden (2 decks) and Spanish 21. All of them are good, in particular Downtown Vegas and Atlantic City where you can double down on any first two cards. The decks are not shuffled after every hand, which is a big plus.

Global Player offers a multi-player experience, as well as a form of help screen which questions your strategy if it thinks you've made a playing mistake and would like the opportunity to change. That's a nice player-friendly feature.

The video poker could very well be the best you'll find on the Internet. The Jacks or Better game has a full (9/6) paytable and offers a 4,500 coin jackpot for a Royal Flush. I don't believe I've seen that on a paytable in the real world come to think of it. In addition to fair paytables, you'll find perhaps the best and broadest selection of games. This is a must stop if you fancy video poker.

This site is a haven for roulette players, too. It offers two versions of the game (American and French). The French version with the single zero makes it your game of choice. This, plus the ease of play and the graphics, make it the most entertaining online roulette game. The "en prison" rule is in effect, too, which lowers the house edge even more. A nifty little feature is the option to click on the announces box and you'll be able to place your bets that way. It lists some intriguing roulette wagering methods you may not even have been aware of.

Jazz Casino and Sportsbook
(www.jazzcasino-sportsbook.com)

This is a brand new entry into the online casino market, which probably goes against my tried and true rule, but the fact that it is operated by a well-respected Costa Rican casino owner makes it worthy of your inspection. With a reputation to uphold, I don't think this site would run bad games.

Certainly the six-deck blackjack and the stingy rules are no lure, but the craps offers double odds and you can play for a dollar minimum. The Jacks or Better, Deuces Wild and Joker Wild video poker games appear to have promise. My guess is that this site is going to be around for a while and attract a good following.

Lasseters On-Line Casino
(www.lasseters.com.au)

The site is under the supervision of the rules and regulations enforced by the Australian government, which is your online guarantee that the games are fair and honest and the payback percentages are true. I didn't care for the blackjack game, but the roulette is the single-zero European version.

Most of what this site has in its favor is its Australian roots. On the less than favorable side, there is not a big selection of games and I found that it wasn't a real pleasurable playing experience.

The River Belle Casino
(*www.riverbelle.com*)

I really like the playcheck feature on this site. It enables you look at a complete record of all the bets you make, including time, amount bet, the cards involved in the play, and the result. It serves as a nice personal record as well as a safeguard for safe and responsible play.

The blackjack is single deck, but they shuffle after every hand; you can double only on 9-10-11, and you can't double after splits. I don't recommend the single-odds craps game, but the roulette is the good European brand with the single zero.

Gold Club Casino
(*www.goldclubcasino.com*)

There are two very good reasons to check out this site: craps and blackjack. The online craps is a rare three-times odds version of this popular game, and the blackjack is the single-deck variety.

Island Casino
(*www.islandcasino.com*)

Don't visit this site for the craps (single odds on the dollar game) or the video poker (Jacks or Better in the anemic 8/5 version), but you may want to take a look at the blackjack which is available in single-deck, six-deck and Spanish 21 versions. The graphics are no great shakes, but the rules are: dealer stands on all 17s, double on any first two cards, and double after splits. The shuffle in the six-deck game occurs about halfway through, generous for an online game.

Pai Gow Poker at the Island Casino is attractive, too, especially if you want to learn what the game is all about.

Where to Log on for Information

As I have already established, there is precious little objective information available for Internet gamblers. Until the government enacts legislation and wraps cyber gambling in a package of safeguards and regulations, the burgeoning industry is forced to police itself. But there are places for you to go to find solid information. Here are some of them:

Interactive Gaming Council
(*www.igcouncil.org*)

The Interactive Gaming Council (IGC) is an international trade association committed to the advancement and success of the interactive gambling industry. Its members have a vital stake in the future of the industry, so this organization is intent on providing quality controls in order to maintain the integrity of Internet gambling. Seeking to ensure that the people who utilize online casinos have a safe and honest experience, and providing the industry with a degree of legitimacy is what the IGC is all about.

When you log onto the Interactive Gaming Council site, you'll read what the organization is about, the services it provides, as well as receive a listing of, and the links to, its current members. There is a consumer complaint form as well as e-mail and telephone contacts.

You can be reasonably assured that members of the IGC have conformed to a list of criteria and are in some way responsible and accountable for the manner in which they conduct business. There is a "Seal of Approval" program also to be implemented that will further enhance the credibility of member organizations.

I would encourage you to look for ICG members when you are seeking an Internet gambling site. You'll find the notation on the opening page of member sites. Eventually you'll also be able to look for the seal of approval. With the hundreds upon hundreds of sites out there, and with consumer protection guaranteed by no one, it makes sense to look for sites that, for the lack of a higher authority, are at the very least accountable to fellow members of the industry to ensure their integrity.

Safe Bet
(*www.safebet.org*)

This fledgling organization bills itself as a nonprofit, independent Internet casino-testing laboratory that monitors online casinos. An IGC member, Safe Bet offers a membership program for online casinos and sports books. Be aware that it was formed in 1998 by a group of software developers, so again we're talking about an internal policing organization, but for lack of any outside security force, it remains a site that you can turn to when it comes to exploring safe Internet gambling avenues.

The purpose of Safe Bet is to protect users through the regular testing of online casinos. They do this through the use of 10 Standards of Fairness:

1. *The casino must continue to pass random, mathematical tests of their gaming software (a criteria which applies to Platinum and Gold certified SafeBet sites but not to the lowest level it categorizes, Silver members).*

2. *All games must accurately play by the posted rules.*

3. *If there is a free version of the game software, it must play by the same rules and odds as the real money version.*

4. *All claims of odds and payout percentages must be true.*

5. *Any simulation of a real-world gaming device, such as cards or dice, must statistically behave precisely the way that device would in real life.*

6. *All wagers must be protected in the case of power failure or player disconnection.*

7. *Sufficient cash reserves must be maintained to pay winners.*

8. *Play disputes must be handled efficiently and accurately.*

9. *Complete logs must be maintained of every player transaction and game.*

10. *Players must always have the right to speak with a casino representative about their account.*

If you look for the SafeBet seal on an Internet gambling website, the organization assures that the participating site has had its games subjected to testing by SafeBet's team of mathematicians.

Once again there are no bona-fide assurances, but a visit to the SafeBet pages and a tour of its member casinos can be a rewarding experience in a cyber jungle.

The GameMaster
(*www.gamemasteronline.com*)

An outstanding site for online gamblers or anyone who has thought about gambling online. It's packed with information about online gambling, includes links to Las Vegas pages, and has many other resources you'll find helpful and interesting. There are also strategies and graded reviews of online casinos as well as a blacklist of sites on which players have encountered problems. Some of the online casino reviews are a little dated, but others have been reviewed and updated with pertinent changes. This is a must stop for online gamblers of every interest and level.

Rolling Good Times Online
(*www.rgtonline.com*)

A wealth of information for gamblers of every level and means. The site includes industry news, a selection of columns from America's top gambling writers including Frank Scoblete, John Robison, Henry Tamburin, Walter Thomason, Bootlegger, John Grochowski, John May, Barney Vinson, Alene Paone, Star Brooks, Larry Edell and, yours truly, John Brokopp, among others. There are new articles posted on a daily basis, along with numerous links to sites that are of interest to gamblers. A special feature for enthusiasts of online gambling is a review section of selected Internet casinos that offers complete and thorough analysis of every aspect of play on the particular site.

The Wizard of Odds
(www.thewizzardofodds.com)

Although this site accepts advertising, I found it to be a very valuable resource for gamblers of all types, including Internet casino players. There is a great deal of helpful information, including statistics about game odds, probability and tidbits about specific sites and software providers. There is something for everyone interested in gambling.

GamblingLicenses.com
(www.gamblinglicenses.com)

The site describes itself as the starting point for Internet casino and sports-betting operators seeking an interactive gambling license, but it also can prove to be an informative resource for players. You'll be able to see a listing of all the gaming software and system providers with links to their websites. You can also access a database of Internet gambling license holders around the globe.

Where to Go for Thoroughbred Racing Information

The Internet has become "Horse Player's Heaven" for all people who take their handicapping seriously. At the mere touch of a button a whole world of information is opened up, much of it free of charge or available at a nominal fee.

There are a few quality, highly reputable information sources that present a veritable treasure trove of all the information that you need to become the most well-informed horse player you can be. Most of the sites have links to other sites that will prove to be invaluable when it comes to uncovering winners.

Unlike gathering information on casino gambling on the Internet, which is unregulated and, for the most part, fragmented, horse racing info is thorough, concise and easily attainable. What's more, you can bank on the databases you utilize to be trustworthy and accurate.

Daily Racing Form
(www.drf.com)

The words on the print version of thoroughbred horse racing's "bible" say it all: "America's Turf Authority Since 1894." Generations of horse bettors wouldn't even think about making a bet without first consulting the trusted pages of the "Form." Now the venerable publication is setting the pace in online racing information.

The site has undergone numerous changes in its short history and currently ranks as one of the most comprehensive sites you can log onto for any and all information you need as it pertains to any race track in the country. For example, as a free service, you can set up your own homepage and receive information that you yourself select according to region, even specific tracks. You can also access complete, daily entries from every major track in the nation. Charts and past performances are available for subscribers.

Other features include live odds on every major track in North America, plus this invaluable perk—targeting specific horses, trainers and even *types* of races at tracks around the country. If your handicapping specialty is allowance races on the turf, therefore, you can access a daily listing of all such races being run at tracks around the country. You'll also be kept up to date with news as it happens, including injury reports, stakes starters, and next probable engagements for the country's leading horses.

An ideal companion resource for this site is the *Daily Racing Form*'s print edition called *Simulcast Weekly*. It includes handicapper's diaries that list track trends and biases, trip notes, and commentary from trackmen at major tracks. It also lists winners from every track in North America and *Horses to Watch* selected by on-track, everyday expert observers. There are plenty of jockey and trainer stats with patterns to key on as well.

Equibase
(www.equibase.com)

The Equibase Company, based in Lexington, Kentucky, is the thoroughbred-racing industry's official database for racing information. The website offers a complete menu of all the racing information you need. What's more, the site is easy to navigate and many of the valuable services it provides are available for a modest fee.

There is a place to click on to obtain the current carry-over pools of exotic bets at tracks around the country, if those happen to be your handicapping specialty. A new addition to the site is "Backstretch Buzz," a first hand, eyewitness compilation of notes, information and insight provided by Equibase employees who staff the tracks.

You'll be able to purchase race programs, *Daily Racing Form* past performances, and such handicapping services as selections by the experts, *ClassGraph* and *SpeedGraph*. Also for sale are complete charts of every race and complete individual track statistics. The free services that are available nationwide include official entries, in-today lists, workouts, late scratches, track changes, cancellations and a results ticker.

Also available from the Equibase website is a "Virtual Stable" feature that allows you to create a stable of your favorite horses to watch and then receive free notification of when and where the horses are running, workout reports and race results.

You can also link to the websites of tracks around the country as well as access information from individual tracks through the Equibase site.

Bloodstock Research Information Services
(*www.brisnet.com*)

Here you'll find a cornucopia of information that will also get you quite heavily into the breeding and pedigree aspect of the sport. The information available can prove valuable for handicappers who target 2-year-olds and early season maiden races in which there is no traceable form.

In addition to tracking horses through their pedigree, Bloodstock Research Information Services also offers thorough start-by-start, career histories of individual horses as well as recent horses for a reasonable fee. A "Super Tote" setup is also available which enables handicappers to receive real-time odds for selected tracks, 60-second updates, program pages, pools, results, scratches, weather and exotic pools and payoffs. Now that's a complete service in any handicapper's book!

The site has a comprehensive list of member services that will give you—at a finger's touch—your complete account status. There are also program and past performance lines, as well as charts and results. You can also pay for expert handicapper services that cover the thoroughbred world, as well as professional sports selections and a *Las Vegas Football Review.*

One invaluable feature on this site is the availability of handicapping software that you can download. The software includes various handicapping systems based on factors such as fractional times, odds and even one that includes what's defined as inferential handicapping which puts maiden and turf races in the spotlight in an attempt to uncover betting value.

Thoroughbred Track Websites

The individual thoroughbred racetracks around the country have not been left behind when it comes to keeping in step with the times. Most of them have information-packed websites that will keep interested bettors posted with all the up-to-date happenings on the particular circuit in question.

In this modern era of selective handicapping, and all the new windows of opportunity that have been opened up to handicappers through simulcast and Internet wagering, visiting these individual sites is a must for any long distance handicapper who wants to be as informed as he or she can possibly be.

If you live in the Chicago area, for example, but are a devotee of the thoroughbred races at Santa Anita in Southern California, you can log on to *www.santaanita.com* and be enriched with jockey and trainer standings, press releases, late changes, track conditions, weather and a great deal more information that's personalized to that track.

Handicappers of out-of-town tracks are no longer restricted to the past performance lines of the horses they are interested in. The Internet has made it possible to visit every track via the magic of cyberspace. Some of the last minute information you'll be privy to can make the difference between winning and losing. It can certainly give you an advantage over those who are too lazy, or simply not inclined to go that extra mile, when it comes to picking a winner.

Here are the Web addresses of some of the major tracks around the country:

Aqueduct Race Course
www.nyracing.com

Arlington Park
www.arlingtonpark.com

Bay Meadows Race Course
www.baymeadows.com

Belmont Park
www.nyracing.com

Beulah Park
www.beulahpark.com

Calder Race Course
www.calderracecourse.com

Canterbury Park
www.canterburypark.com

Churchill Downs
www.churchilldowns.com

Del Mar Thoroughbred Club
www.delmarracing.com

Delaware Park
www.delpark.com

Delta Downs
www.deltadowns.com

Ellis Park
www.ellisparkracing.com

Emerald Downs
www.emeralddowns.com

Evangeline Downs
www.evangelinedowns.com

Fair Grounds
www.fgno.com

Fairmount Park
www.fairmountpark.com

Fingerlakes
www.fingerlakesracetrack.com

Fonner Park
www.fonnerpark.com

Golden Gate Fields
www.ggfields.com

Great Lakes Downs
www.greatlakesdowns.com

Gulfstream Park
www.gulfstreampoark.com

Hawthorne Race Course
www.hawthorneracecourse.com

Hialeah Park
www.hialeahpark.com

Hollywood Park
www.hollywoodpark.com

Hoosier Park
www.hoosierpark.com

Keeneland
www.keeneland.com

Laurel
www.laurelpark.com

Lone Star Park
www.lonestarpark.com

Louisiana Downs
www.ladowns.com

Meadowlands Racetrack
www.thebigm.com

Oaklawn Park
www.oaklawn.com

Penn National
www.prrc.com

Philadelphia Park
www.phonebet.com

Pimlico Race Course
www.pimlico.com

Portland Meadows
www.portlandmeadows.com

Prairie Meadows
www.prairiemeadows.com

Remington Park
www.remingtonpark.com

Retama Park
www.retamapark.com

River Downs
www.riverdowns.com

Rockingham Park
www.rockinghampark.com

Ruidoso Downs
www.ruidownsracing.com

Sam Houston Race Park
www.shrp.com

Santa Anita
www.santaanita.com

Saratoga
www.nyracing.com

Sportsman's Park
www.sportsmanspark.com

Suffolk Downs
   www.suffolkdowns.com

Tampa Bay Downs
   www.tampadowns.com

The Ontario Jockey Club (Woodbine)
   www.ojc.com

Thistledown Race Course
   www.thistledown.com

Turf Paradise
   www.turfparadise.com

Turfway Park
   www.turfway.com

Let It Ride.com
(*www.letitride.com*)

This site puts you in touch with thoroughbred racing on a global scale. It isn't necessarily for followers of the sport in North America, but if you want to keep up with what's going on in Europe, Australia and other parts of the globe, this can be a wonderful resource for you. Don't forget, the annual Breeders' Cup, as well as Grade I turf stakes in the United States, have combined to give thoroughbred handicapping an international flair. If you want to keep up with the leading horses across the ocean as well as news and stakes results, Let it Ride.com opens many doors.

Handicapper's Daily
(*www.handicappersdaily.com*)

This is a tried-and-true site that's geared toward handicappers looking for that extra edge you may not find on similar sites. For example, you can keep up with some of the new spins that the nation's racing secretaries are putting on race conditions, an often-overlooked feature of handicapping. It's no secret that there are races written with the express intent of luring particular horses. If, in fact, a particular horse uniquely fits an oddball condition, it can be a signal that a solid bet is in the offing. By directing at least a portion of your attention to race conditions and knowing when and how to pick up on conditions that are out of the parameters of what is considered everyday or normal, you can capitalize on rare wagering opportunities that the untrained eye will miss.

Other highlighted features on *Handicapper's Daily* include expanded and improved workouts plus links to handicapping services. Stats and info on the site are provided by Equibase so you know you can't go wrong.

Thoroughbred Times
(*www.thoroughbredtimes.com*)

Thoroughbred Times.com is the online version of the venerable print edition, a weekly publication that serves as one of the thoroughbred industry's top trade publications that has wide readership among fans and horsemen alike. This is the kind of site you want to go to if you want to be fully informed about everything that's going on in the racing world from a news standpoint. The site is updated throughout the day to keep you posted on late developments, such as injury reports and regional situations that can have an impact on your last-minute handicapping decisions.

There is also a news archive and links to related thoroughbred sites. This is the kind of site you'll want to turn to during the days leading up to nationally prominent stakes races, such as the Triple Crown and Breeders' Cup events.

Blood Horse
(*www.bloodhorse.com*)

Another online version of one of the thoroughbred sport's oldest and most reputable weekly trade publications.

It's an all-encompassing site with a wealth of horse racing links, a listing of valuable web resources, and a thorough compilation of stats from around the country and individual tracks. The news and updates will make you a well-rounded and knowledgeable handicapper. Blood Horse is one of those "go to" sites if you want a stepping stone to anything and everything about the thoroughbred sport.

TrackMaster
(www.trackmaster.com/advantage)

TrackMaster is another handicapper's resource that provides statistical information for a minimum charge at the touch of a mouse click. It's an Equibase company that provides official Equibase speed, pace and class figures as well as TrackMaster's proprietary Power Ratings accessible in PDF format.

Expanded TrackMaster Plus features to the site include expanded race records and statistics, jockey, trainer and pedigree information, as well as horse, jockey and trainer notes. TrackMaster was well respected on its own even before it became an Equibase company. It can be money well spent if you want to go that extra step for information, especially if you don't have the time to juggle stats and figures yourself.

Youbet.com
(www.youbet.com)

America's premier online wagering provider continues to get better and better. When Youbet.com reached an agreement with Television Games Network (TVG), it opened up betting horizons at tracks that had previously been blacked out, including such powerhouse tracks as Churchill Downs, Hollywood Park, Keeneland, Belmont and Saratoga. It also opens up the chance for Youbet.com to accept wagers on the Triple Crown and Breeders' Cup races.

Youbet.com, which was launched in 1998, accepts wagers from the residents of 39 states. It is looking to expand its base and solidify its position in the fledgling online wagering market.

Youbet.com also offers an express operating system that requires no CD to install and no software to download, a major advancement. Live, streaming audio and online video, along with up-to-the minute information is sent directly over the Web. The fees are minimal; you are given access to all member tracks, complete race programs, odds and instant and secure wagering through Ladbrokes in Pennsylvania, plus handicapping resources.

PlayboyRacingUSA.com
(www.playboyracingusa.com)

Penn National Gaming signed a deal with Playboy Enterprises early in 2001 to build an online pari-mutuel wagering site called PlayboyRacingUSA.com. Penn National Gaming handles the complete day-to-day operation while Playboy provides the marketing, branding, user interface, design and content. Since the site is licensed and operated in the state of Pennsylvania, account wagering is legal. Penn National, whose wholly owned subsidiary is eBetUSA.com, gives PlayboyRacingUSA.com the opportunity to offer live racing with wagering at some 30 tracks across North America.

Of course the site will feature Playboy's special brand of entertainment to online horse racing, including Playboy Betting Bunny Deanna, who also is the interactive hostess for PlayboySportsbook.com.

Using Television as an Online Tool

Television is growing as a visual tool that new millennium handicappers can use in conjunction with their online wagering experience. Handicappers can learn a lot from what they read but there is much truth to the "a picture paints a thousand words" cliché.

Television Games Network (TVG), based in California, can be logged onto at *www.TVGnetwork.com*. It offers a telephone-wagering account service, but more importantly it is a source to go for racing coverage via the Dish satellite system and local cable.

The Big Boys Get Into the Internet Action

While the federal government hemmed and hawed over the legality of gambling on the Internet, and what kind of legislative and judicial action must be taken regarding it, the state of Nevada, never shy in matters of wagering, has taken the initiative in a bold way. Lawmakers in the Silver State have positioned Nevada on the cutting edge of cyberpower if and when rolling the dice online is declared a legal activity within the boundaries of the United States of America.

In June of 2001, the Nevada State Senate approved, and Gov. Kenny Guinn signed, legislation that will allow Nevada casinos to offer Internet gambling if the practice is made legal in this country. A desire to offer online gambling carries with it a hefty price for the casino owners: There would be a $500,000 licensing fee, an annual renewal fee of $250,000, and a 6.25 percent tax on winnings. The actual licensing is not expected to take place before 2003.

What the bill does do is this: For the first time a government-licensed and sanctioned-licensed regulatory board, in this case the Nevada Gaming Control Board and state Gaming Commission, will make a thorough and detailed study of Internet gambling. This would include suppliers, operations, safeguards, integrity and a host of other regulations governing the proposed operation of Internet gambling sites by Nevada casinos.

That's very good news for Internet gamblers. It could sound the death knell for gambling on Internet sites licensed outside the borders of the United States. It will certainly put suspect operations out of business. Why would anyone want to gamble online on a casino based in the Caribbean when they could gamble with a Nevada casino and enjoy all the protections and assurances that a state regulated enterprise could guarantee? They would also enjoy certain perks that only land-based casinos could offer, such as free stays at the host properties, free meals, shows, etc.

Nevada will proceed full-steam ahead with study groups, including law firms, to analyze the federal laws as they pertain to Internet gambling now and what changes could be in the offing if judicial and legislative changes regarding Internet gambling are in the offing. The future of Internet gambling is getting bigger and bigger.

Glossary

Account: An agreement with a company that permits you to take advantage of the services that it offers.

Activate: To make a window active by clicking on it.

Authentication: The action which allows the user to gain access to a particular computer system, usually through the use of name and password prompts.

Back button: The button on the toolbar which allows you to revisit locations.

Bit: A binary digit, the smallest piece of information that a computer can hold.

Bit rate (bits per second): The rate at which bits are transmitted.

Bookmarks: Permanently stored addresses for sites you want to revisit.

Browser: A software program that allows you to access information on the World Wide Web.

Byte: A combination of bits used to represent a single charac-
ter.

Chat: Communicating with a person, a group or a site on the
Internet in real time by typing on your keyboard.

Click: To press and immediately release the button on your
mouse.

Client: A computer or software program for accessing services on the Internet. The machine or software that provides the service for the client is the server.

Cyberspace: Coined by writer William Gibson, an early term
for the entire world of online information and services.

Default: The value of a configuration option that the software
will use unless the user indicates a different value in
the setup program.

Download: To copy a file from another computer to your own
computer. The opposite of upload.

Domain-name address: The English address of a computer on
the Internet, such as *www.lasvegas.com*, as opposed to
the IP (Internet address) which is a series of numbers
separated by periods.

Drag: To click on something and move the pointer while
pressing and holding a button on your mouse.

E-Mail: Short for electronic mail.

FAQ: Abbreviation for "frequently asked questions."

File: A named collection of information on a disc or other storage device, such as text, programs and graphics.

Firewall: Software or hardware that creates controlled access between an internal network and the Internet.

Forward button: The button on the toolbar which allows you to revisit locations.

Font: The size of displayed and printed characters.

FTP: Abbreviation for "file transfer protocol" which allows you to transfer files from one computer to another.

FYI: Abbreviation for "for your information."

Gopher: A method for organizing information on the Internet.

Hardware: The physical components of a computer, such as hard discs, printers, keyboards, etc.

Homepage: The document you choose to display when you open when you open your Web browser.

Hot spot: Another name for a link.

HTML: Abbreviation for "hypertext markup language" which tells a Web browser program how to display text or graphics.

HTTP: Abbreviation for "hypertext transfer protocol" that Web clients and servers use to communicate with one another. It is the basic protocol for the World Wide Web.

Icon: An image that represents an object such as a file.

Internet: A super network comprised of smaller networks that work together to exchange information using a common set of rules for communication, or protocol. The Internet is distinguished from the World Wide Web in that the Internet is like highway and the World Wide Web is a vehicle that uses the highway to get from destination to destination.

Internet Service Provider: A commercial service that provides Internet access to businesses and individuals.

IP Address: The unique digital address for each computer on the Internet.

ISDN: Abbreviation for "integrated services digital network," the standard that makes possible the digital transmission of voice, video, and data over telephone lines.

Java: A program language developed by Sun Microsystems which gives developers the capacity to create object-oriented applications that may be run from within Web browsers.

JPEG: A compressed graphics format.

Kilobyte: Two to the tenth power bytes of data. A 64k file, for example, contains 65,536 bytes of data.

Link: A word, image or other area of a website that users can click on and move to another area in the document or to an entirely different document.

Log in: The process of identifying yourself to a system by typing in your name and password in order to initiate a session on your computer.

Log off: The process of terminating a session on your computer.

Maximize: To expand a window to its maximum size.

Megabyte: 1,024 kilobytes.

Minimize: To reduce the size of a window, and in some cases, to hide the window until you wish to open it again.

Modem: Short for modulator/demodulator. It's the piece of hardware that connects your computer to other computers using analog telephone lines.

MPEG: A compressed video file format.

Navigation: Browsing the Web or HTML documents.

Net: Slang for the Internet

Network: A set of interconnected computers.

Offline: When your computer is not connected to the Internet.

Online: When your computer is connected to the Internet.

Pixel: The smallest unit of graphic information on a computer screen.

Pointer: The icon that moves on your computer screen when you move the mouse, such as the arrow, hand or I-beam.

Print button: The button on the tool bar that allows you to print a document.

Protocol: Rules of interaction among computers that allow for the exchange of information.

Random Access Memory (RAM): Computer memory that temporarily stores information. The more RAM your computer has the better.

Read-Only Memory (ROM): Computer memory that cannot be changed by the user and remains even when the computer is turned off.

Rich text: Text that contains HTML or some other variety of special formatting.

Scroll: To look through the contents of a document not currently displayed.

Search engine: A program on the Internet, such as *www.yahoo.com*, *www.altavista.com* and *www.excite.com*, that users access to search for information online.

Server: A computer or program that provides information or services.

Service provider: A commercial organization that provides connections to the Internet.

Software: File or files that contain information that will tell the computer what to do.

Stop button: A button on the toolbar that permits the user to cease downloading a file.

Surf: Slang for using a browser to move through the World Wide Web.

Toolbar: A row of buttons that provides easy access to sets of controls.

Upload: To send a file from your computer to another computer. The opposite of download.

URL: Abbreviation for "uniform resource locator." It's the process for creating addresses for the World Wide Web by uniquely identifying a Web page. A URL consists of three parts: a protocol tag such as http, a server name such as lasvegas and a directory path such as .com.

Web- Short for World Wide Web.

Web page: A document on the World Wide Web written in hypertext.

Website: A collection of pages on the World Wide Web.

World Wide Web: The interconnected set of hypertext documents maintained on computers called servers located throughout the Internet. The servers send the documents to your computer.

WWW: Abbreviation for the World Wide Web.

Index